SHONEN JUMP MANGA EDITION
NARUTO
VOL. 31
FINAL BATTLE
STORY AND ART BY
MASASHI KISHIMOTO

CHARACTERS

Sakura
サクラ

チヨ
Granny Chiyo

Naruto
ナルト

Gaara
我愛羅

Kakashi
カカシ

Itachi
イタチ

The Story So Far…

Naruto, the biggest troublemaker at the Ninja Academy in the village of Konohagakure, finally becomes a ninja along with his classmates, Sasuke and Sakura. During the Chûnin Selection Exams, Orochimaru and his henchmen launch *Operation Destroy Konoha*. Naruto's mentor, the Third Hokage, sacrifices his own life to stop the attack, and Tsunade becomes the Fifth Hokage. Lured by Orochimaru, Sasuke leaves Konohagakure. Naruto fights valiantly against Sasuke, but cannot stop his friend from following the path of darkness…

Two years pass, and Naruto and his comrades grow up and undergo separate training programs, until Gaara falls into the hands of the Akatsuki. Naruto charges into the enemy's lair to rescue Gaara, but Deidara stops him. Sakura and Granny Chiyo remain in the cave locked in battle with Sasori!!

NARUTO

VOL. 31
FINAL BATTLE

CONTENTS

Number 272: Granny Chiyo vs. Sasori...!!

KASHAK

READ THIS WAY

!
WHUP WHUP WHUP WHUP
SKRR
FUP
HMPH...
WHUP WHUP WHUP

SCREECH
!
KLAK

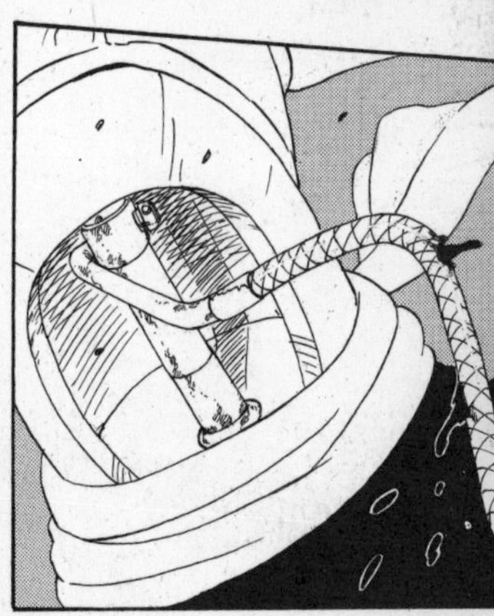

UNH!

SAKURA?!

TAKE THIS!
CHUNK
!

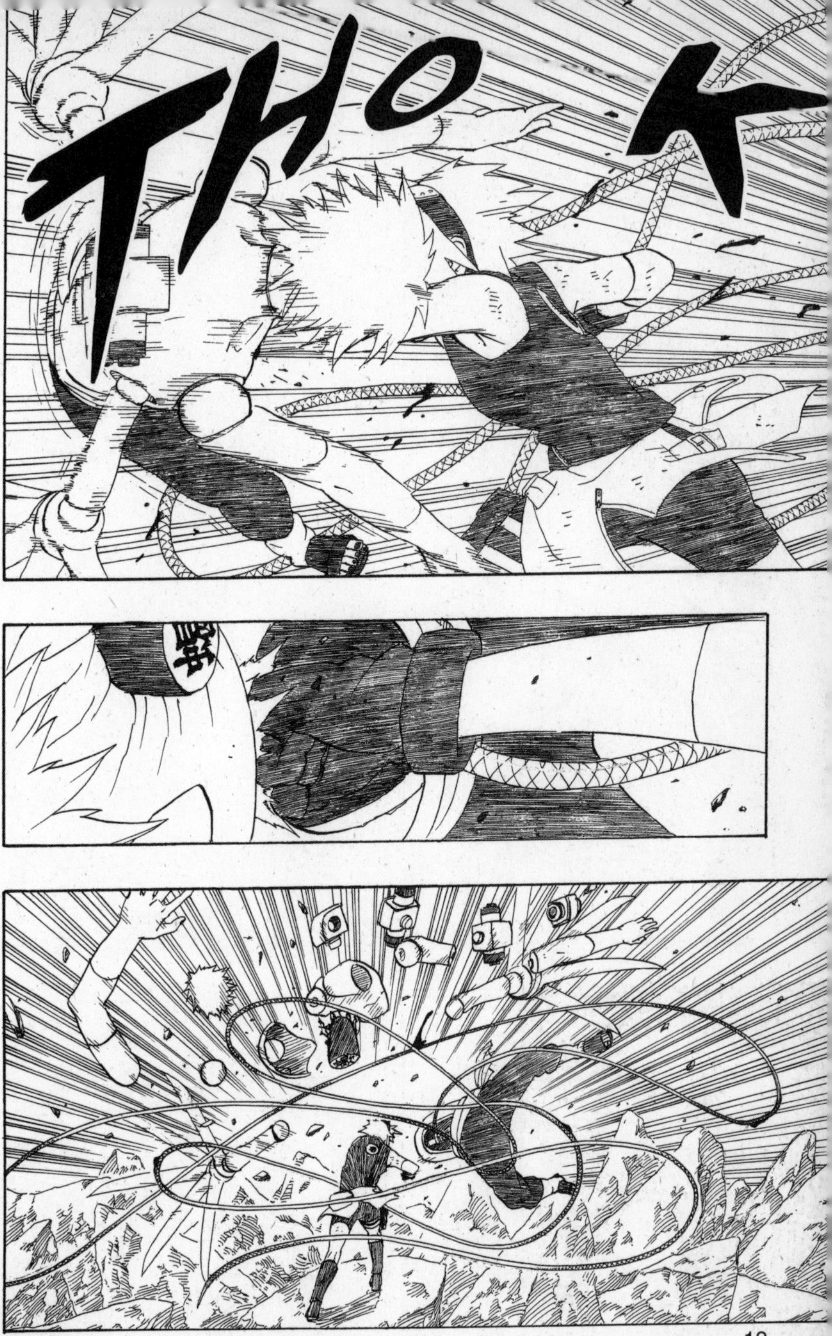

THOCK

READ THIS WAY

RATTLE RATTLE
HUF
HUF

ZOOM

I BEAT HIM... WITH BARELY ENOUGH TIME TO SPARE...
HUF
HUF

HA HA...
I DID IT... GRANNY CHIYO, I DID IT!

SAKURA... YOU...

...
KA CHAK

KLIK KLIK KLAK

!!

...!

READ THIS WAY

SHF
LET'S END THIS HERE AND NOW...

SHUU
FWOO
...

OUT-STANDING, GRANNY.
A PUPPET MASTER'S SKILL IS MEASURED...
...BY THE NUMBER OF PUPPETS THEY CAN USE.

SO... SO MANY...
GRANNY CHIYO'S SECRET, YUBI NO KAZU! MULTIPLE DIGITS...!!
I'VE HEARD OF IT...
YOU ONCE DESTROYED AN ENTIRE FORTRESS WITH IT...

SECRET WHITE MOVE! CHIKAMATSU'S TEN PUPPETS!!

THE FIRST PUPPET MASTER...
...MONZAEMON'S TEN MASTER-PIECES.

SPAK

FWAP
CHAK

YOUR COLLECTION IS QUITE IMPRESSIVE...
BUT...
KLAK

FWOOSH

FWAA

I DESTROYED AN ENTIRE COUNTRY WITH THESE.

?!

...
HE'S DEVELOPED ...SO MUCH...

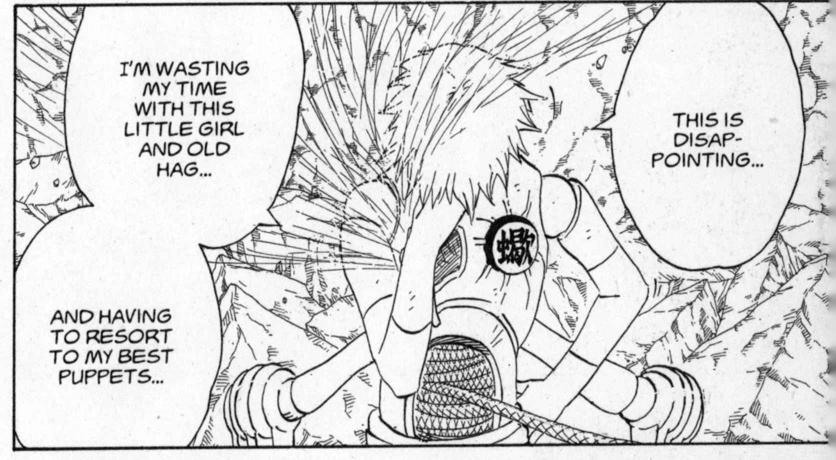
THIS IS DISAP-POINTING...
I'M WASTING MY TIME WITH THIS LITTLE GIRL AND OLD HAG...
AND HAVING TO RESORT TO MY BEST PUPPETS...

SECRET RED TECHNIQUE! PERFORMANCE OF A HUNDRED PUPPETS...!!
IT'S SHOW TIME.

ZOOM
!
SKIDD

...

SAKURA...
!

YOUR ANTIDOTE HAS WORN OFF... STAY BACK.

...

GRIN

?!

YOU ALREADY KNOW, DON'T YOU...?
...WHO I'VE BECOME!

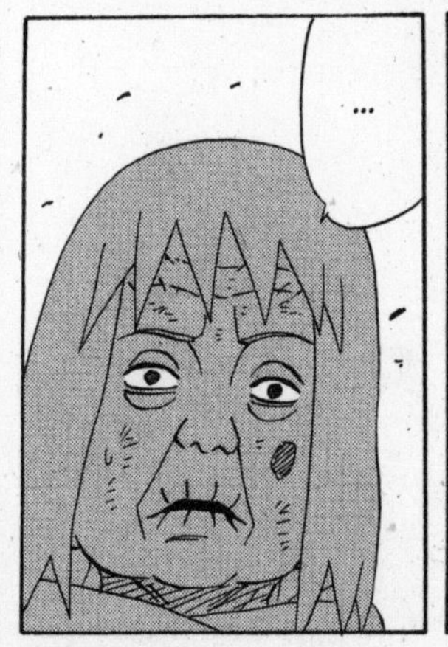
...

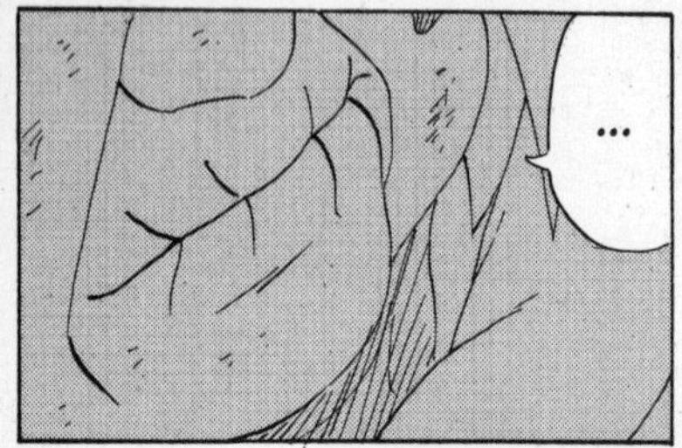

NOW COMES THE FINALE.

READY?

YEAH!

NARUTO

Number 273: Final Battle...!!

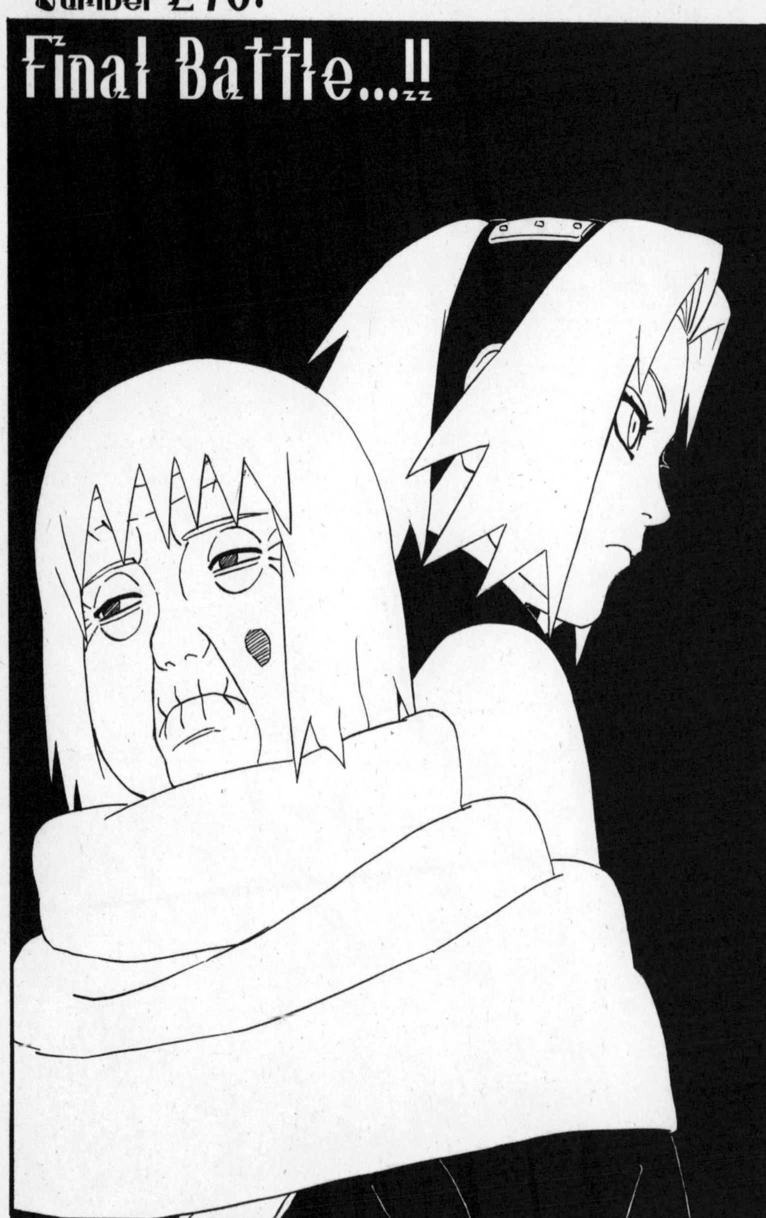

FWWWW
HERE THEY COME!
FWOOSH

FWIP
KLAK
CHAK
CLICK
VVVNN

VWMM
ZOOM
KLANG
SPLEK
SHAK SHAK SHAK

THUD
KA
THP THP
SS SHAK

(Butsu: Buddha)
(Pou: Dharma)
(Sou: Monk)

THOOOM
SQUELCH
!
THERE'RE TOO MANY OF THEM!!

BOOM
HUF
HUF
KLAK
KLAK
SHF
BAM
SKF
FWIP

ONLY ONE ANTIDOTE LEFT... IF EITHER OF US TAKES DAMAGE WE'RE IN TROUBLE.
!!
SLASH
OOF!
...
OH NO...!
FUP
WHOOSH
KREE
!
GRANNY CHIYO!!

BAM

HUF
SAKURA, AIM FOR SASORI...
I'LL TAKE CARE OF THE OTHER PUPPETS.
HUF

OKAY!

USE THIS!
SHF

ZOOM
!
PONG

READ THIS WAY

BLOOP
BOOF
!

READ THIS WAY

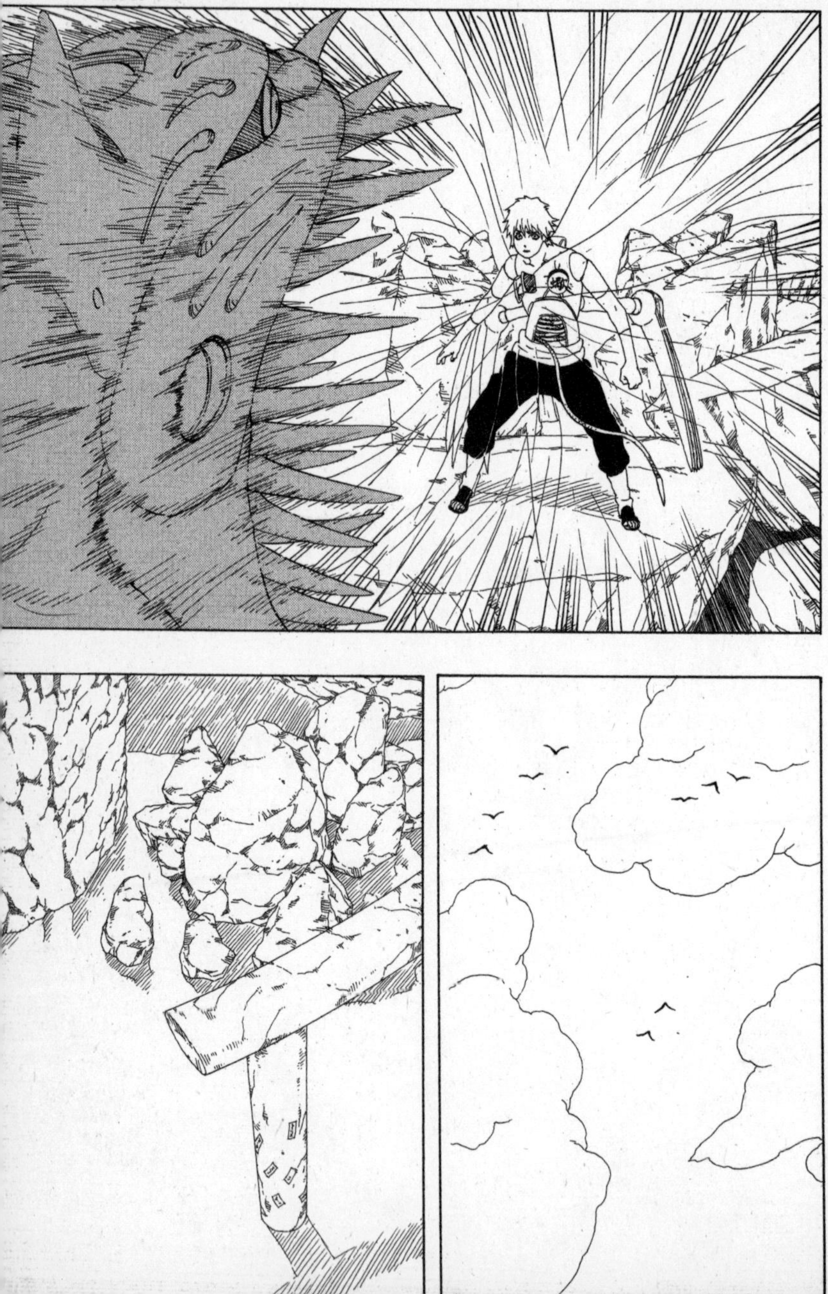

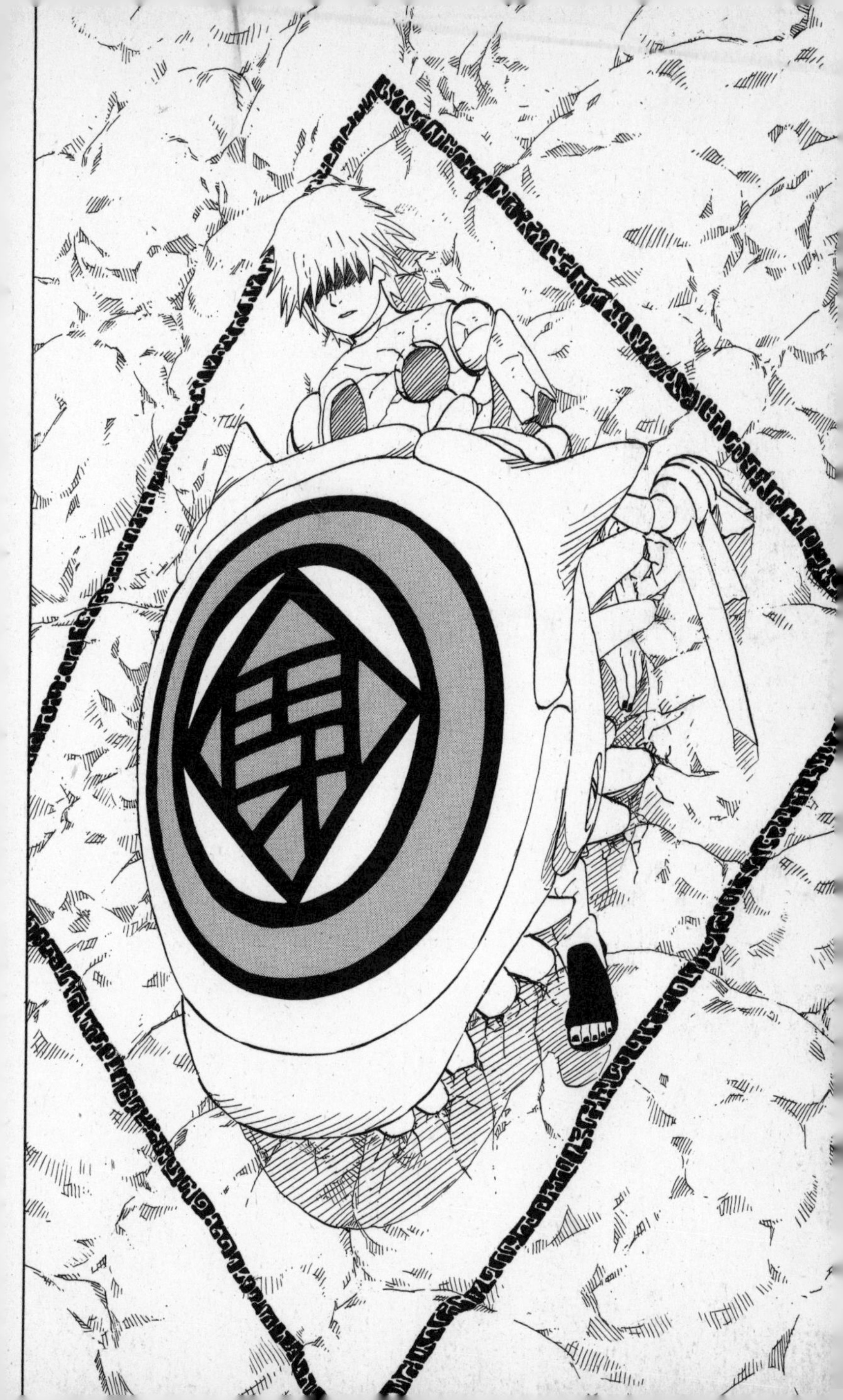

HUF
HUF
I DID IT...

...HE CAN'T MOVE...
...IT'S OVER... SASORI...
THAT SEALING COMPLETELY TRAPS CHAKRA...
YOU CAN'T USE YOUR CHAKRA STRINGS ANYMORE.

ZOOM
GRANNY CHIYO!!
STAGGER
UGH...

TAKE THE ANTIDOTE NOW!

KLAK

KACHAK

READ THIS WAY

FWOO
SH

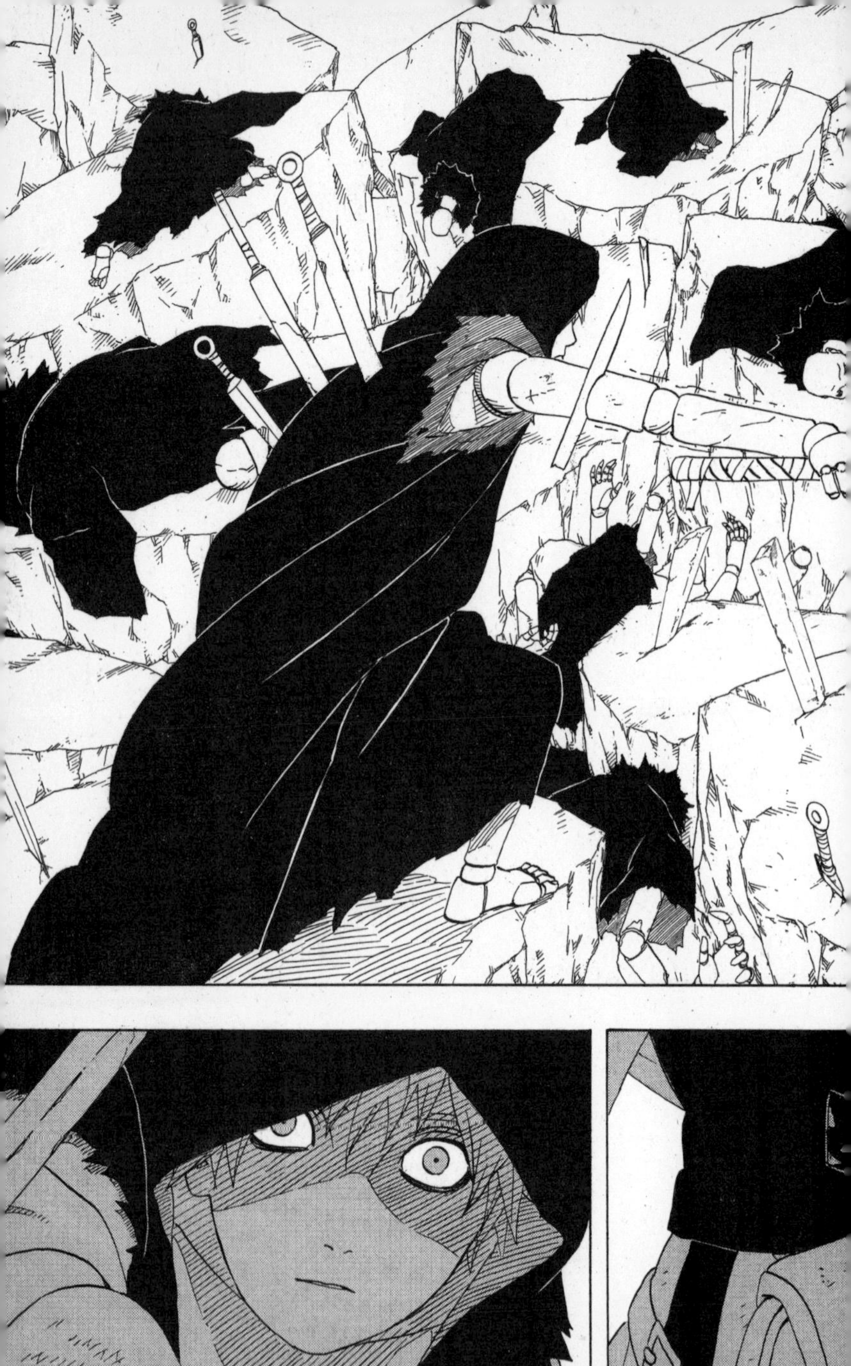

NARUTO

Number 274: Impossible Dream

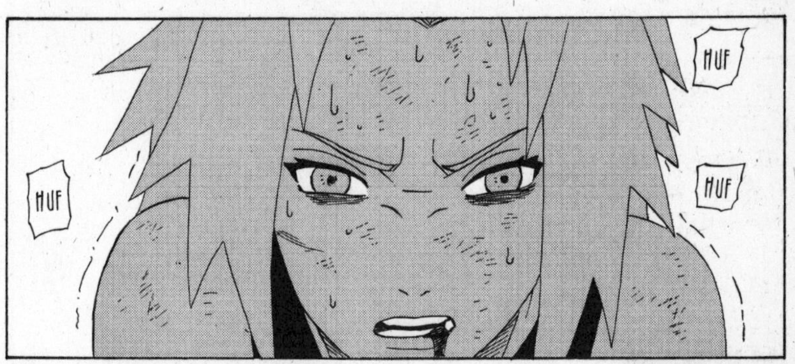
HUF
HUF
HUF

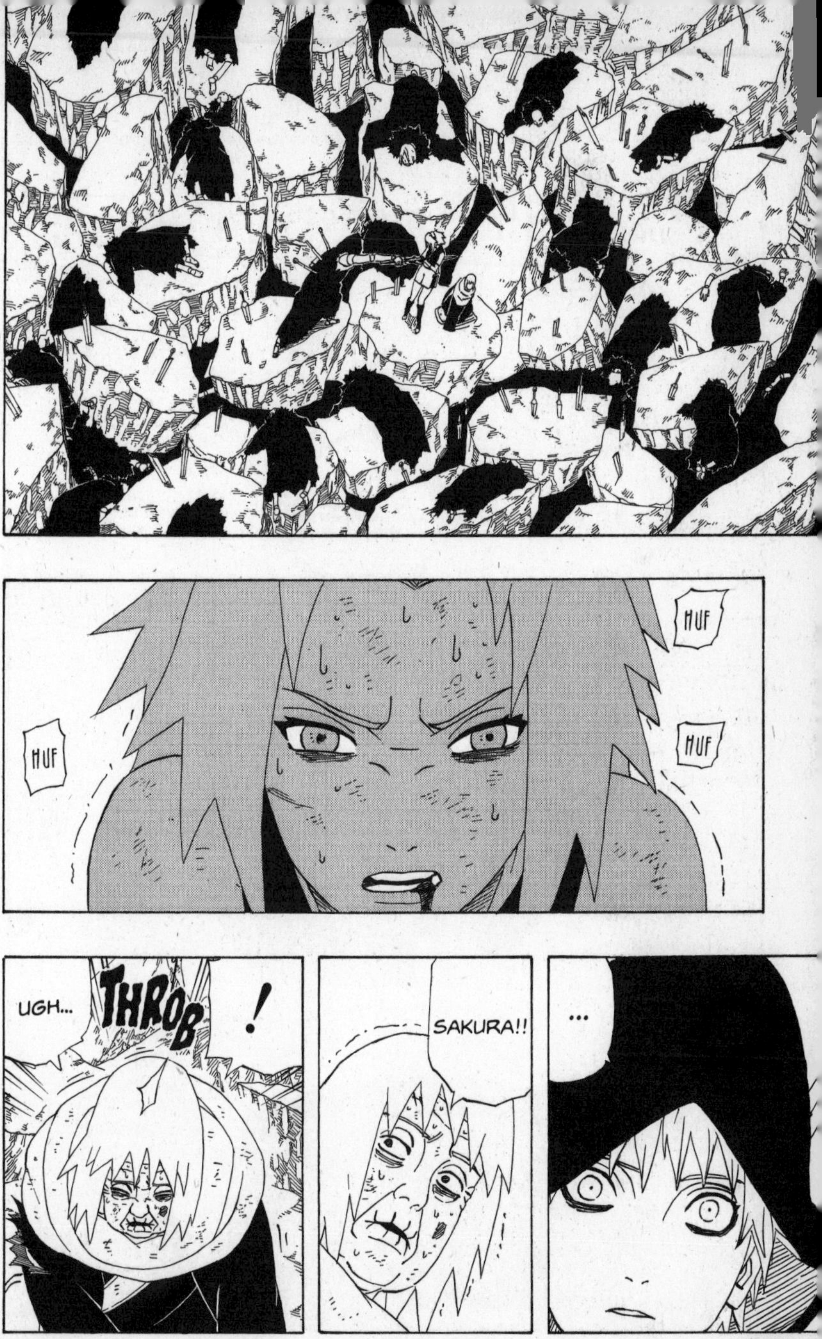

...

SAKURA!!

UGH...
THROB
!

READ THIS WAY

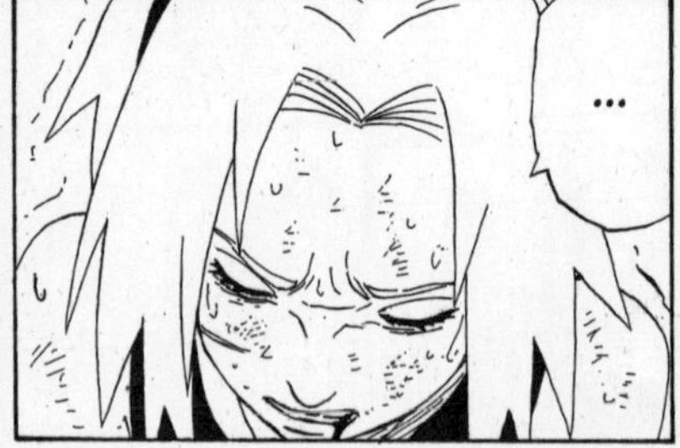

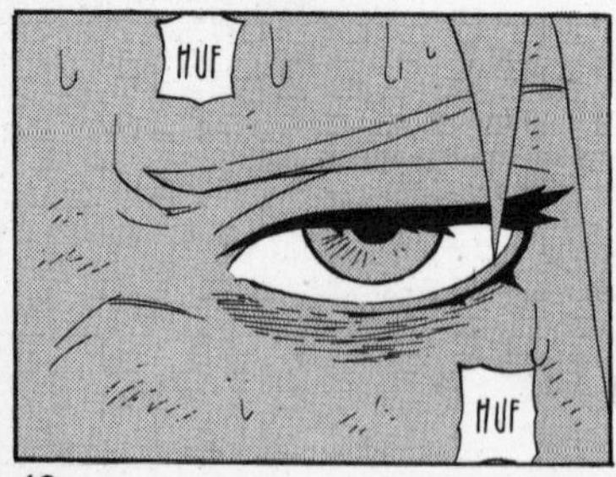

FSSSS

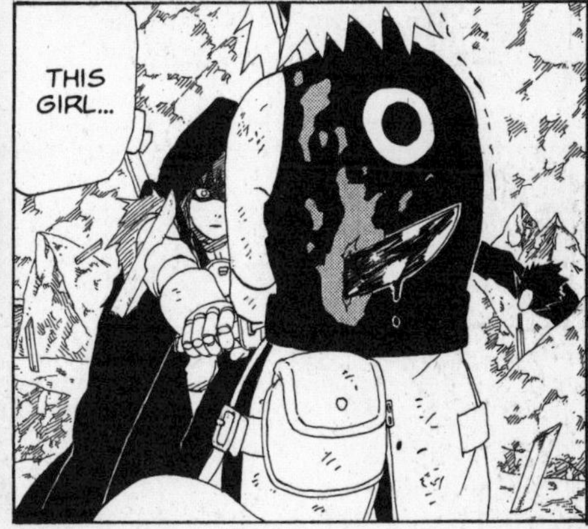
THIS GIRL...

SHE'S STOPPING THE BLEEDING AND HEALING THE WOUND WITH THE SWORD STILL INSIDE HER...
...SUCH SKILL.

!

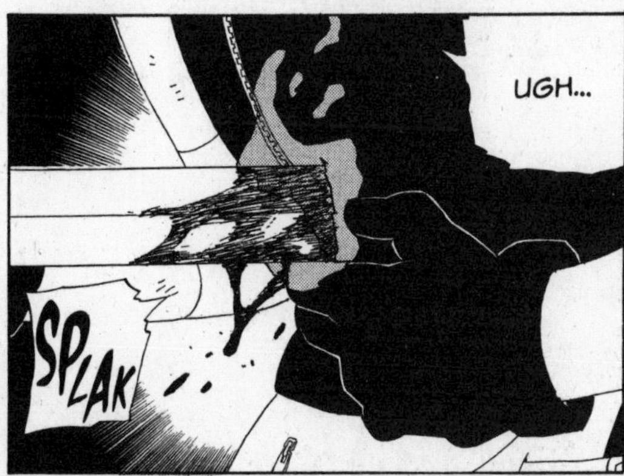
UGH...
SPLAK

READ THIS WAY

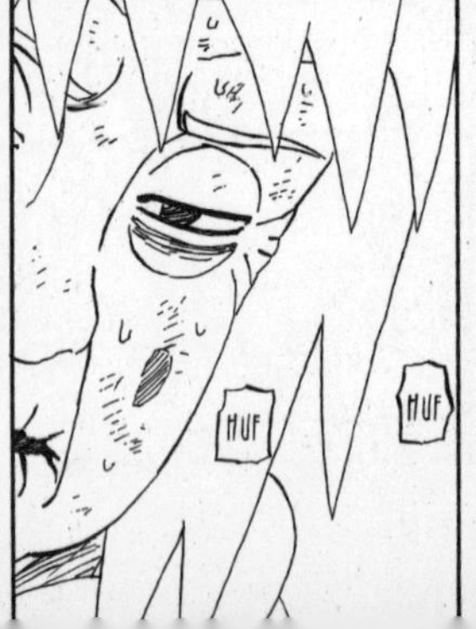

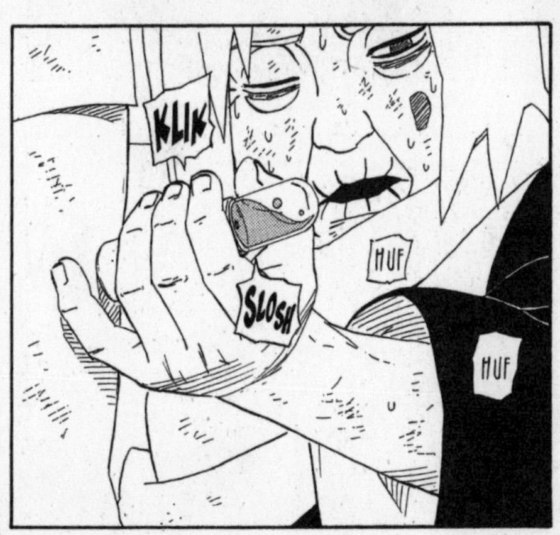
KLIK
SLOSH
HUF
HUF

...

READ THIS WAY

...

I WON'T LET GO.

KACHAK

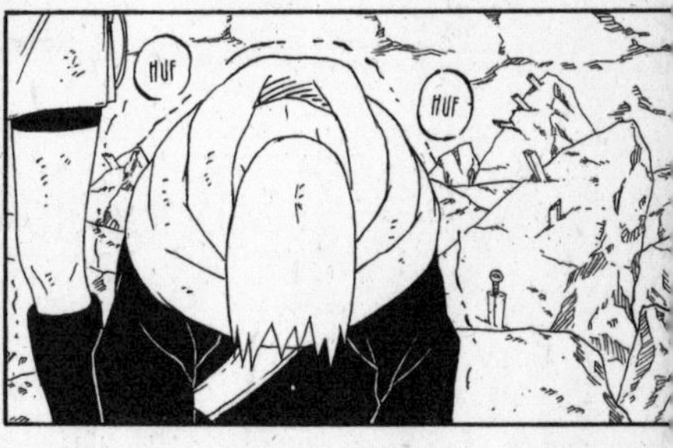
HUF
HUF

GRANNY CHIYO!

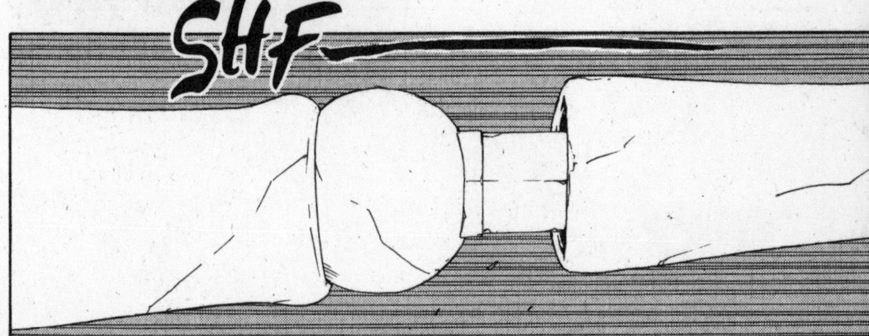
SHF

SWISH

WHOOSH

RATTLE

FWIP

ZOOM

SHAK

READ THIS WAY
HUF
HUF
!

YOU LOWERED YOUR GUARD AT THE LAST MOMENT... SASORI...

YOU CAN'T MOVE ANYMORE...
...CAN YOU...?
HUF
HUF

EVEN THOUGH YOUR BODY IS NOW THAT OF A PUPPET...
...YOU STILL NEED A HUMAN PART TO CONTROL CHAKRA.

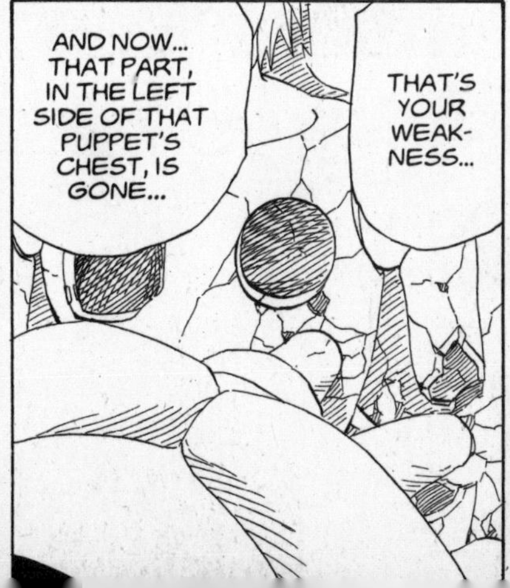
THAT'S YOUR WEAK-NESS...
AND NOW... THAT PART, IN THE LEFT SIDE OF THAT PUPPET'S CHEST, IS GONE...

READ THIS WAY

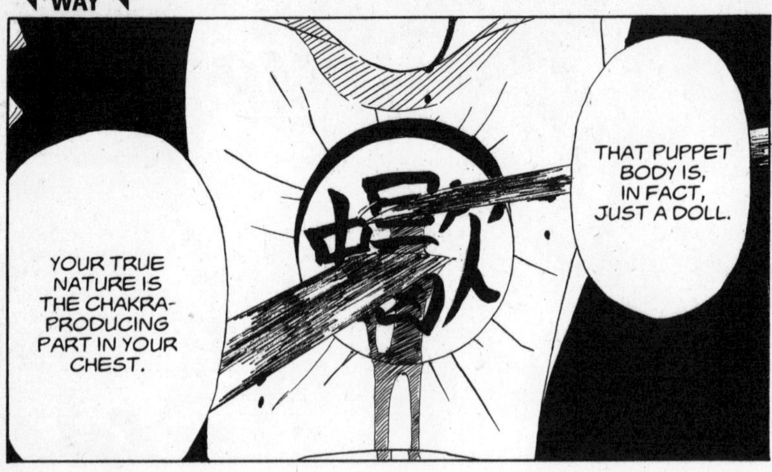

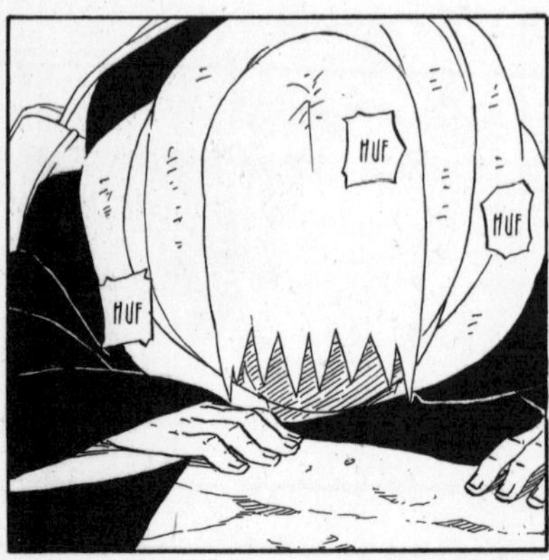

SLUMP
SAKURA!

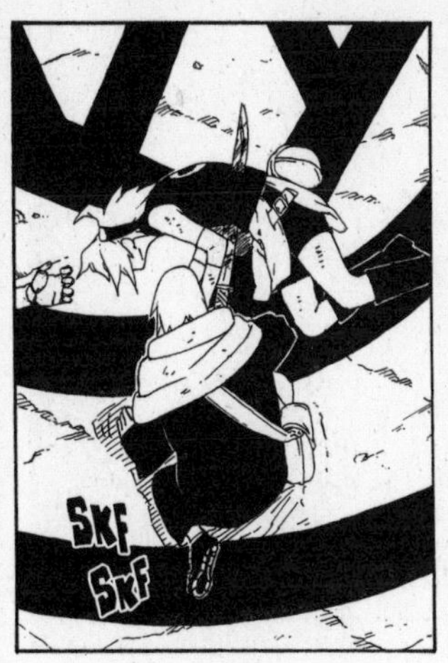
SKF
SKF

GLUG
GLUG

I HAVE TO CLOSE THE WOUND...
...WHILE PULLING THE SWORD OUT.
HUUUM
HUF
HUF

HUUUM

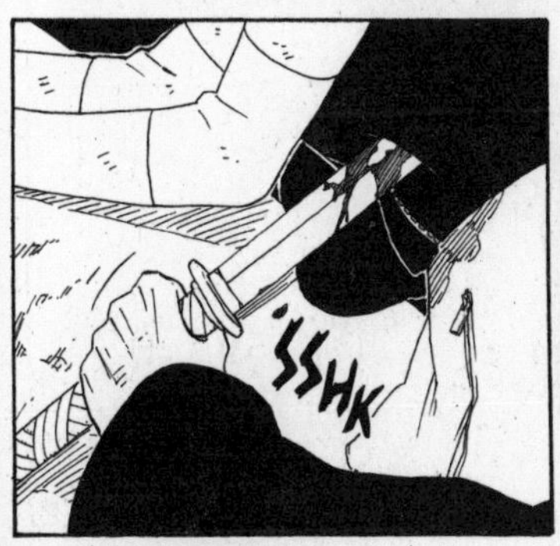
SSHK

UGH...
ZING

STAY WITH ME...
ALMOST... GOT IT...

KLANK -KLANK

FSSSS

IMPOSSIBLE... I HIT A VITAL POINT.
EVEN WITHOUT THE POISON, SHE'S GOING TO DIE.
SHE'S LOSING TOO MUCH BLOOD.

YOU'RE ALSO A MEDIC NINJA...
SO I AIMED FOR A SPOT YOU CAN'T HEAL VERY EASILY.

HMPH... I'VE ALREADY DONE FIRST AID WITH MEDICAL NINJUTSU.
THIS IS NOT MEDICAL NINJUTSU...

?
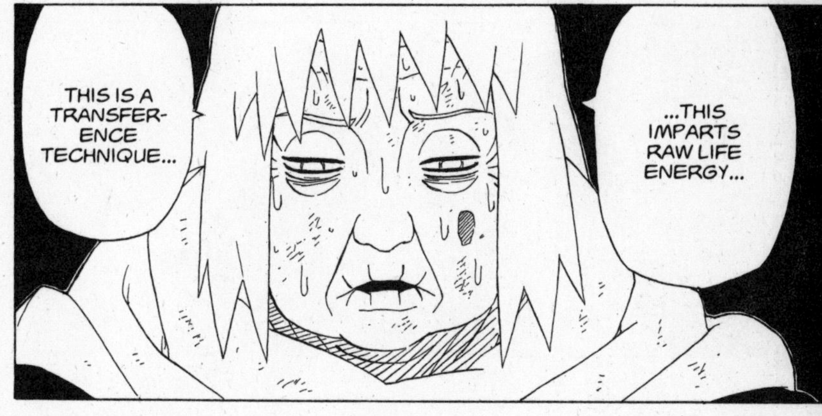
...THIS IMPARTS RAW LIFE ENERGY...
THIS IS A TRANSFER-ENCE TECHNIQUE...
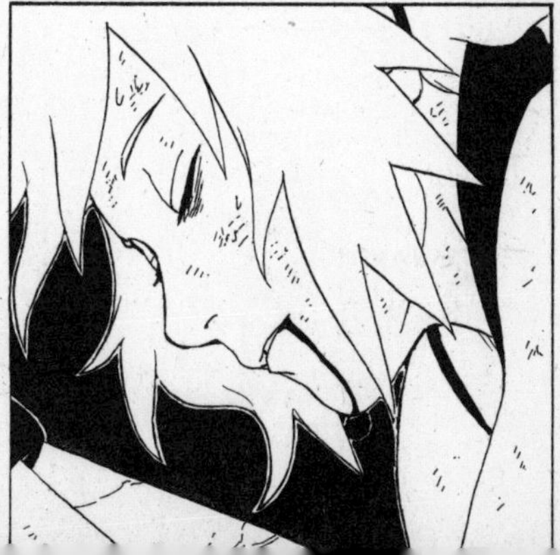
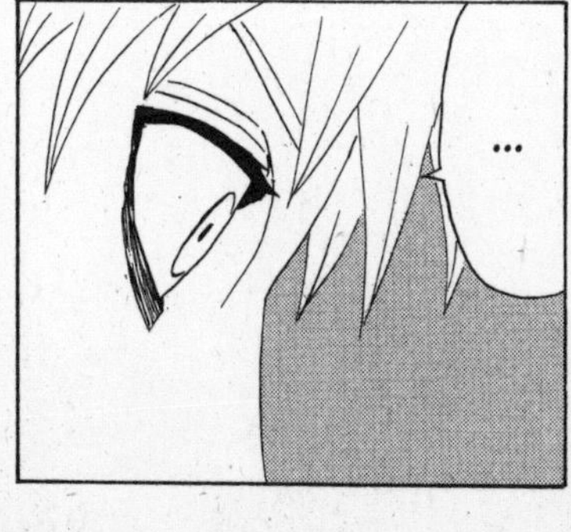
...

READ THIS WAY

...IN EXCHANGE FOR THE LIFE OF THE USER...

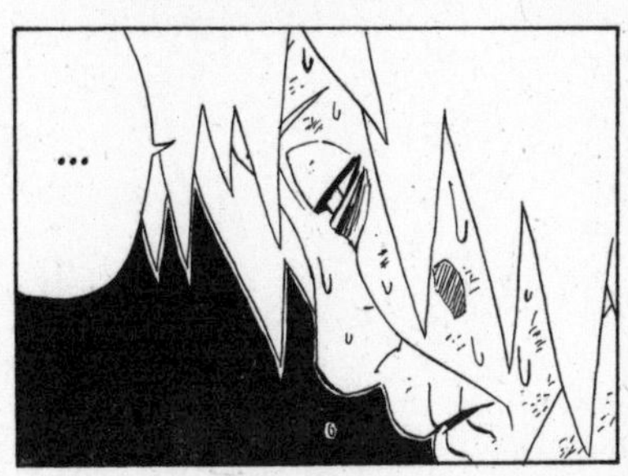

READ THIS WAY

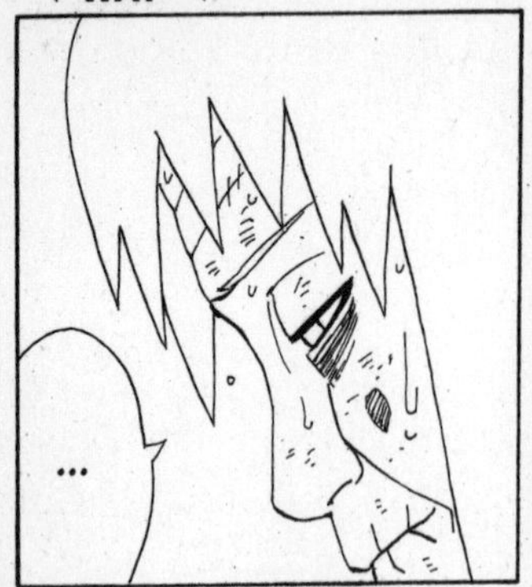

Number 275: Reward...!!

UTTER NONSENSE...

WHEN DID YOU GO SO SENILE, GRANNY?

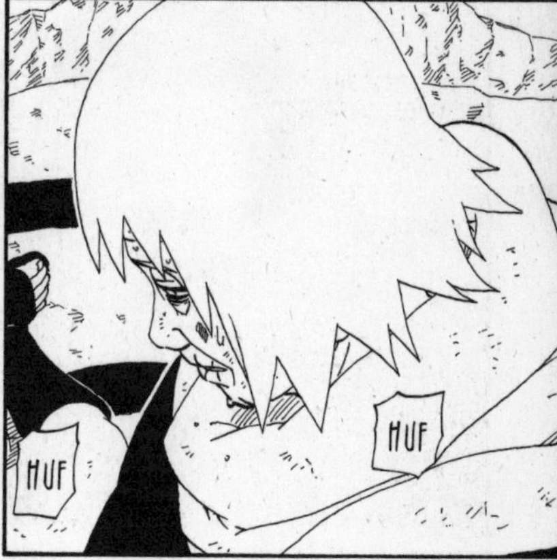

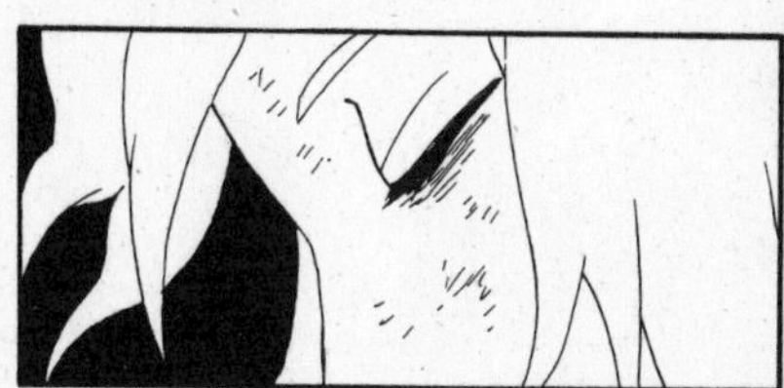

READ THIS WAY

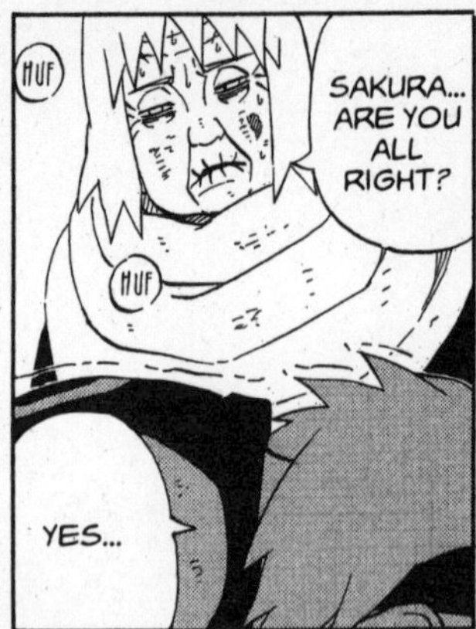

THOK

HUF
HUF

...

YOU'RE WASTING YOUR TIME...
KRIK
YOU'LL ONLY HURT YOUR FIST.
THIS BODY DOESN'T FEEL PAIN.

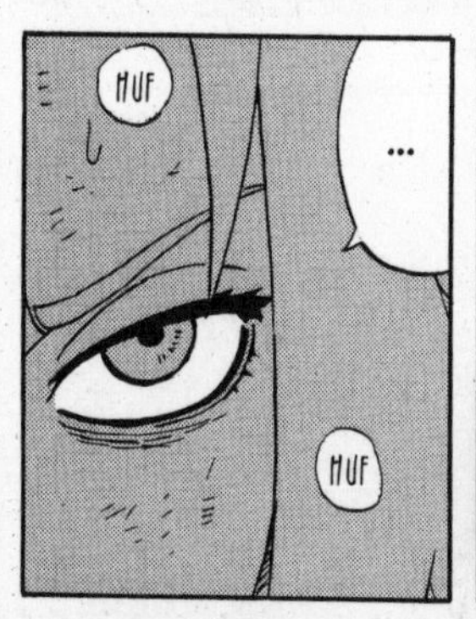
HUF
...
HUF

READ
THIS
WAY

WOMEN... THEY JUST LOVE TO DO...
...COMPLETELY POINTLESS THINGS. HEH HEH...
KACHAK

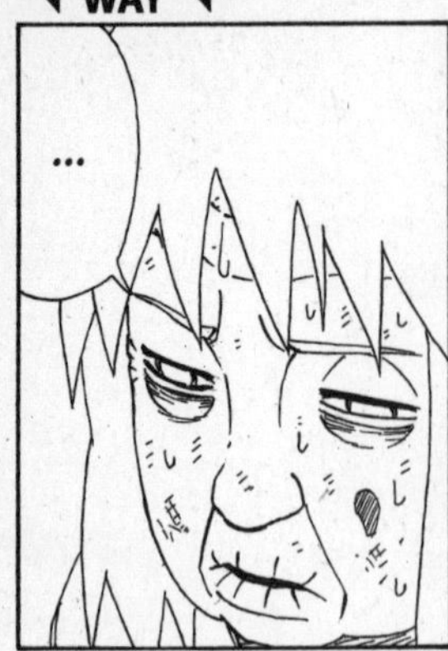
...

EVEN IF MY OWN GRAND-MOTHER DIES...
...I WON'T FEEL A THING.
MY HEART IS...
...JUST LIKE THIS BODY.

SHE'D JUST BE ONE MORE AMONG THE THOUSANDS...
...I'VE KILLED.
THINGS ARE SIMPLER THAN YOU THINK.

SHUDDER
SHUDDER

WHAT DO YOU THINK...
...HUMAN LIFE IS?!

READ THIS WAY

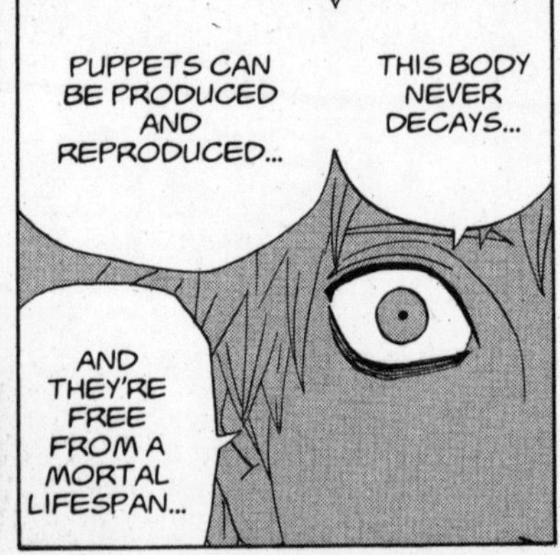

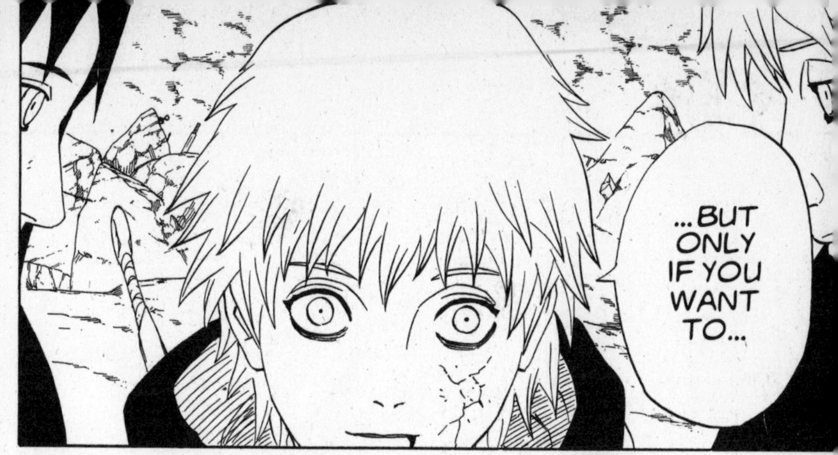
...BUT ONLY IF YOU WANT TO...

...

...BUT IT'S NOT ABOUT QUANTITY...
A COLLECTION IS ALL ABOUT QUALITY.

WHAT ON EARTH...
...ARE YOU...?!

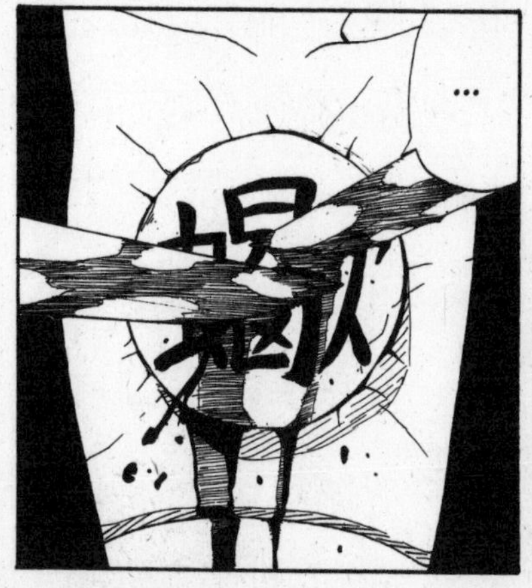
...

READ THIS WAY

SUFFICE IT TO SAY...
...I'M A HUMAN BEING WHO COULDN'T BECOME A COMPLETE PUPPET...

I'M A PUPPET... BUT WITH A HUMAN HEART...
I'M NEITHER HUMAN NOR PUPPET...

...

THE END IS NEAR.
BUT FIRST, I'LL DO SOMETHING POINTLESS TOO...
A REWARD... FOR DEFEATING ME.

...?!

...

YOU WANTED TO KNOW ABOUT OROCHIMARU, DIDN'T YOU?

...GO TO THE TENCHI BRIDGE IN THE HIDDEN GRASS VILLAGE...
...TEN DAYS FROM NOW AT NOON...

WHAT DO YOU MEAN?!

ONE OF OROCHIMARU'S HENCHMEN IS A SPY OF MINE...
I'M SUPPOSED TO MEET HIM THERE...

...!

READ THIS WAY

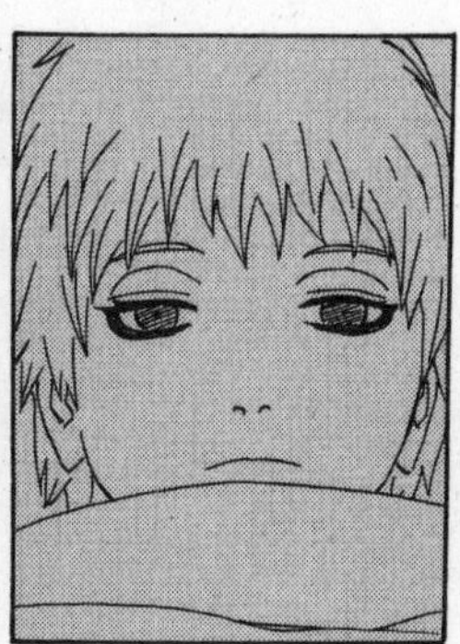

READ THIS WAY

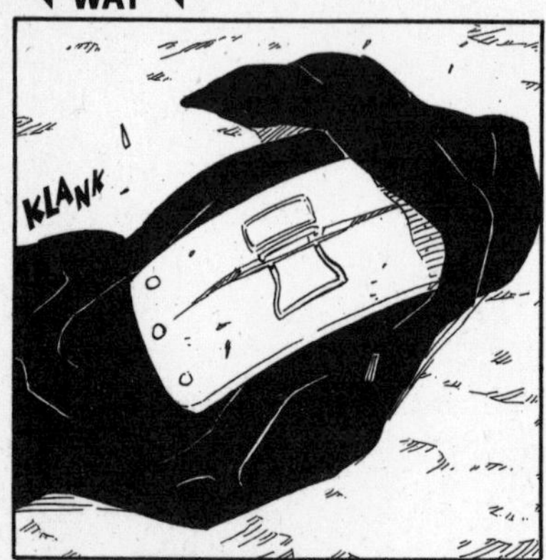

NO...
BY RIGHTS, IT WAS I...
...THAT SHOULD HAVE BEEN DE-FEATED...
?

SASORI ANTICIPATED MY FINAL ATTACK...
BUT... FOR SOME REASON HE COULDN'T DODGE IT.
HE WAS OFF GUARD FOR A MOMENT...

...

...IS THAT...?

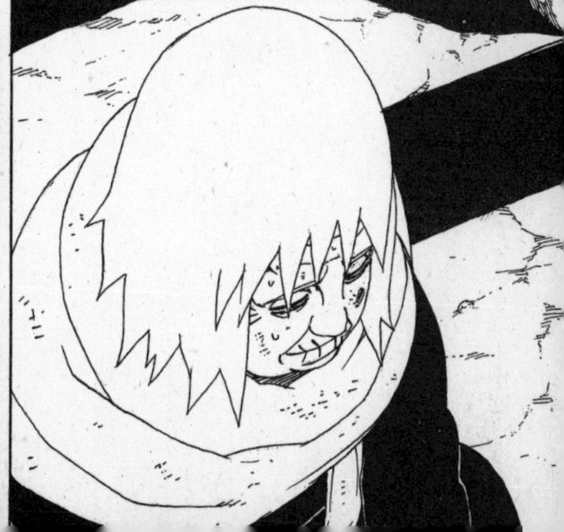

READ
THIS
WAY

!!
UGH...

!
GRANNY CHIYO!

LET'S GET BACK TO THE VILLAGE!
I'LL PREPARE AN ANTIDOTE...
NO...
!

WHY NOT?!
WE'VE DONE WHAT WE HAD TO DO!
WE HAVE TO RETURN TO THE VILLAGE AND COUNTER-ACT THE POISON OR...
INSTEAD OF THAT...
SHF
HUF
HUF

...THERE'S STILL...
...SOMETHING I MUST DO...

MASTER KAKASHI... NOT YET?!

BE PATIENT...

I DON'T HAVE AS MUCH CHAKRA AS YOU...

IT TAKES ME A LITTLE LONGER... BUT...

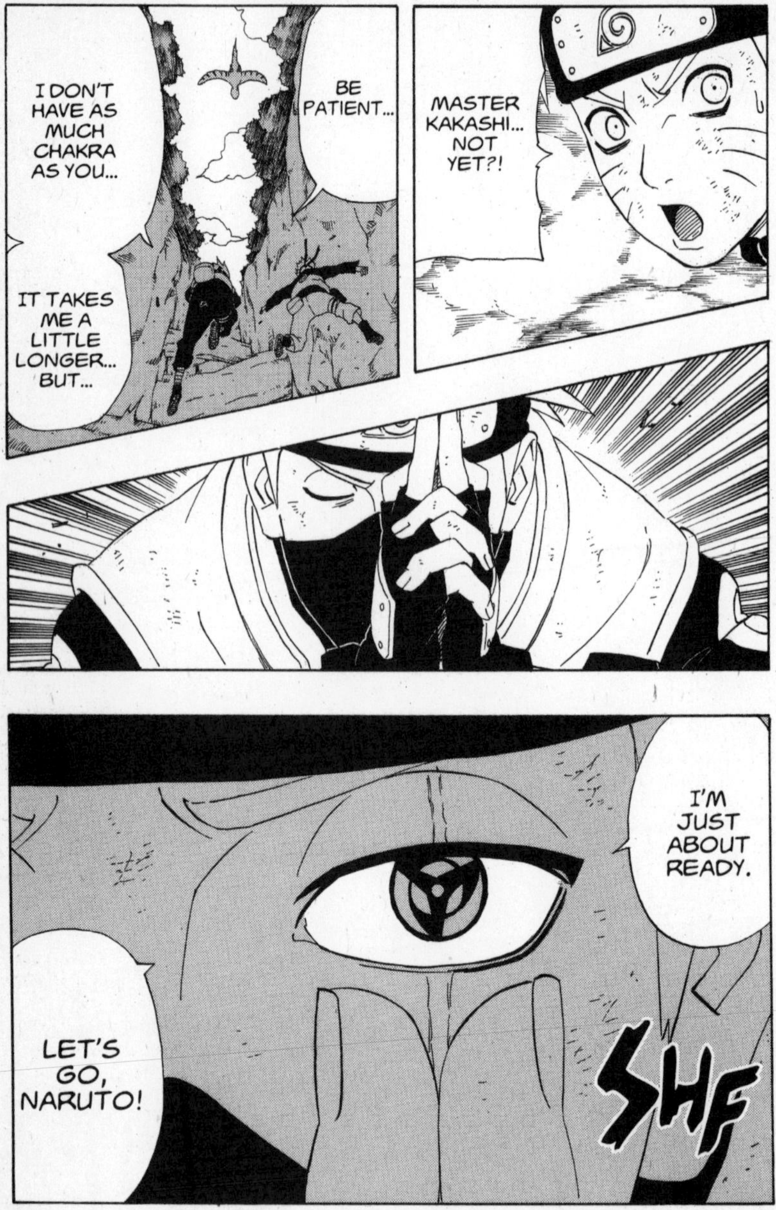

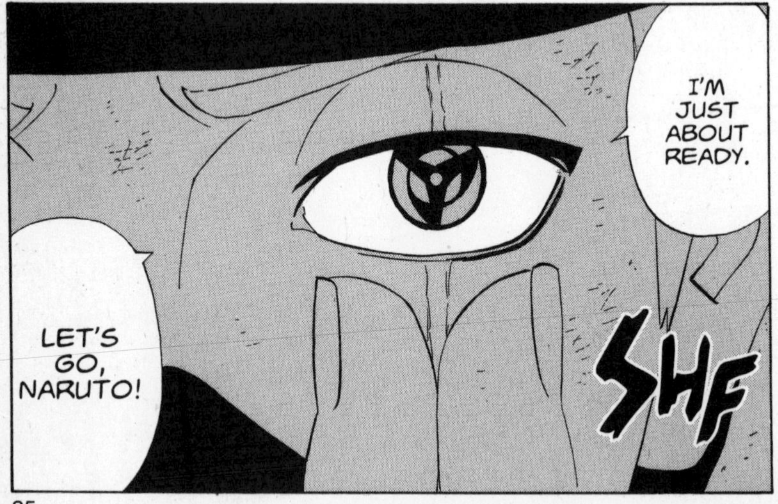

NARUTO

Number 276:
New Sharingan!!

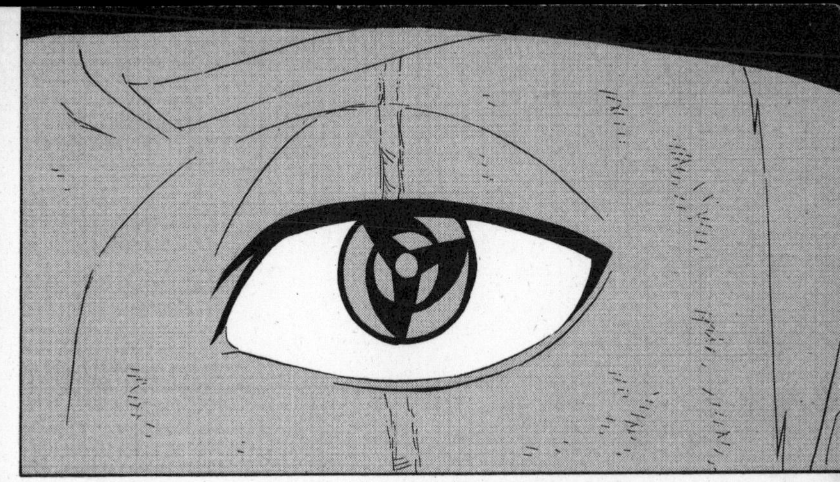

IS THAT...
...WHAT YOU WERE TALKING ABOUT...?

SHOOM
YUP.
A NEW SHARINGAN.

READ
THIS
WAY

...

...
WHAT?

MASTER KAKASHI... IT'S OKAY IF YOU CAN'T...
I'LL FINISH THIS OFF!!

SURE...

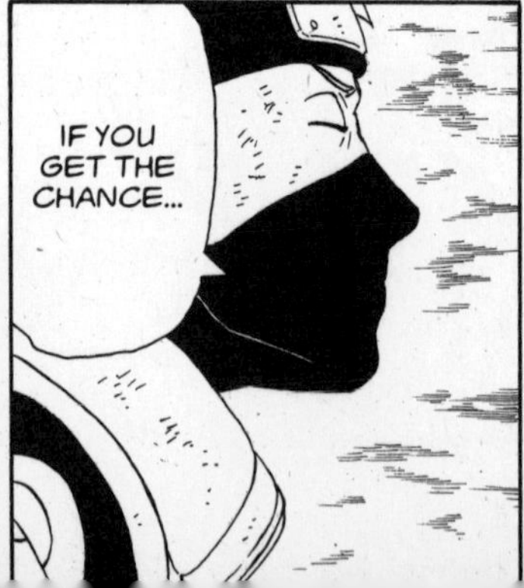
IF YOU GET THE CHANCE...

...YEAH!
TAK

MANGEKYO SHARINGAN !!

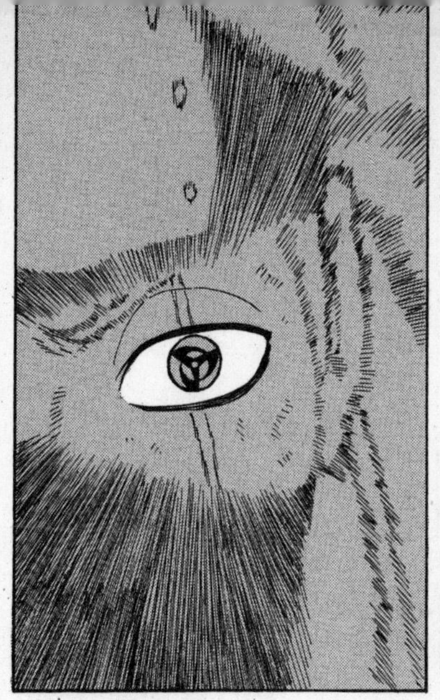

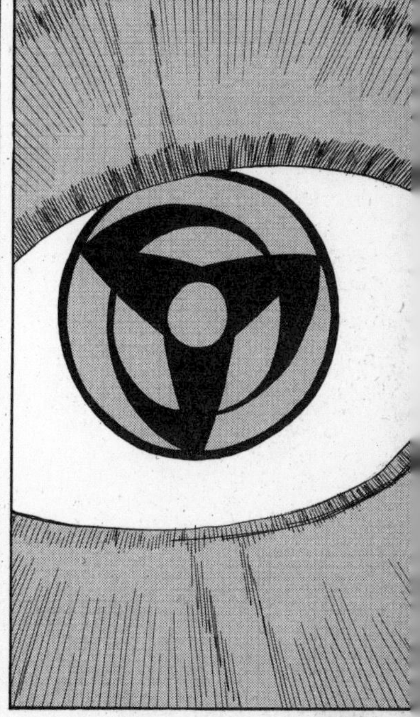

ZZH

ZZZH ZHZH
?!
WHAT... IS THIS?!
ZZH
ZZH !

ZZZH

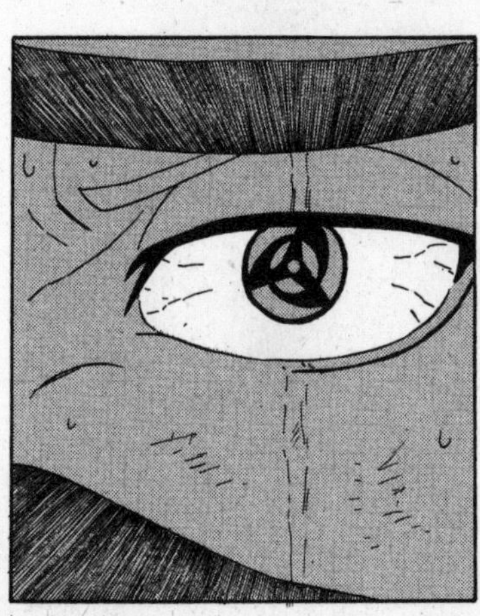

OCULAR JUTSU...?! OH, NO!
FWAP
WOW. THIS JUTSU IS... AWE-SOME...

MY ARM...?!
WHAT IS
THIS?!

UH
OH...

AAARGH!
SPLAK
UGH...
ZZZHZHZH

UNNH...
I MISSED...
I CAN'T PROPERLY CONTROL THE POSITION AND SIZE OF THE BARRIER SPACE.
HUF
HUF
GRRR
ZH
!!
ZZZH

READ THIS WAY

HUF

HUF

ZZH!!

RASENGAN! SPIRAL CHAKRA SPHERE!!
!

READ THIS WAY

ZOOM

BOOM

HUF
HUF
YES!
HUF

TSK...

KAGEBUNSHIN NO JUTSU! ART OF THE SHADOW DOPPELGANGER!!

FWUP

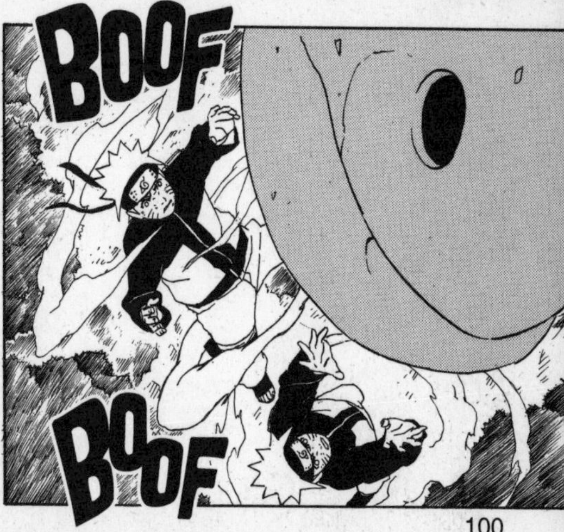

READ THIS WAY

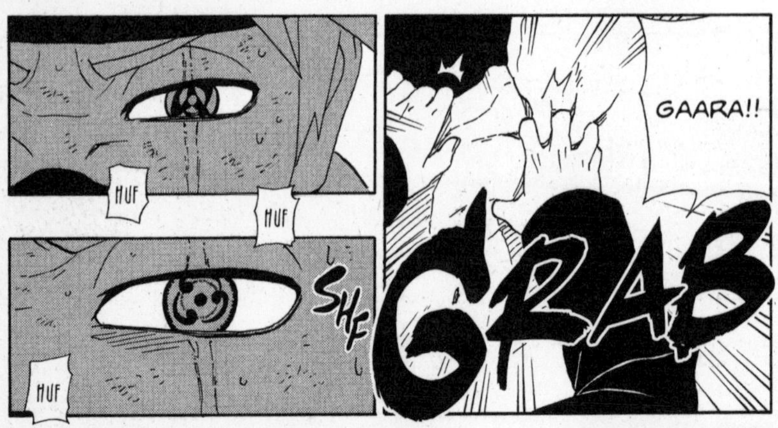

READ THIS WAY

MY RIGHT ARM TOO... I CAN'T USE JUTSU ANYMORE...
...IT'S COME TO THIS... HMMM?

BUT... RUNNING INTO SOMEONE WITH ITACHI-LEVEL OCULAR JUTSU...
THIS JINCHÛRIKI IS NOTHING... THE PROBLEM IS HOW TO DEAL WITH KAKASHI...

IT'S TIME FOR YOU TO GET HIT!

YEAH, YEAH...
I'LL HAVE IT OUT WITH YOU ANOTHER TIME...

YOU'RE TOO CARE-LESS...

DO

Number 277:
The Ultimate Art...!!

BOOF

READ THIS WAY

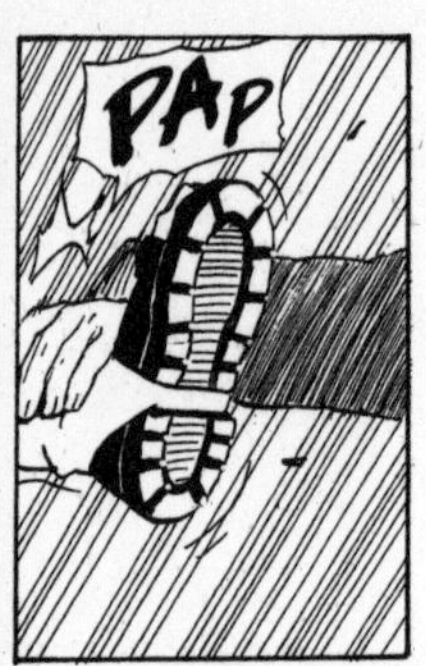
PAP

GRAB

PAP

GRAB

WHOOOO

BAM
ARGH!

SMA
SH
GUF!!
UGH...!
WHAM

DOW
THOK
KRAK
UGH!
AGH!
NGH...!

THOK

NARUTO...

WHAM
!!

CLAY...!
A SUBSTI-
TUTION...?
BOOF BOOF BOOF

GUB GUB GUB GUB

!
THAT'S... WHAT JIRAIYA WAS TALKING ABOUT...

...!
WHAT'S THAT...?
IS THAT THE JINCHÛRIKI...?

TWITCH
GRRRR

TAK
GUB
GUB
GUB

READ THIS WAY

!
GUB
ZOOM
TAK
FWAP
...!
PSSSH

READ
THIS
WAY

HE WAS STRONG ...
HUF
HUF
ALMOST A WORTHY FAKE ME...

ZZZH

HUF
HUF

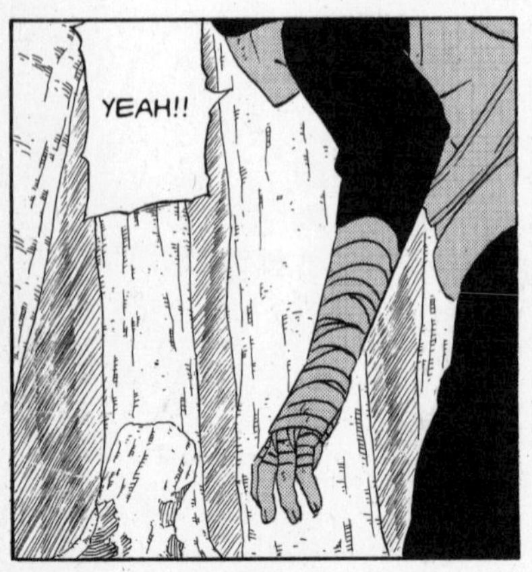
YEAH!!

PHEW ...

ARE YOU ALL RIGHT...? NARUTO...

WHAT...DID JIRAIYA SEE...?
HUF
HUF
SHOOM
!

TAK
FINALLY CAUGHT UP WITH YOU...

!
HOW DID YOU KNOW WE WERE HERE...?
WE SAW THE ENEMY FLY OVER.

IT SEEMS AS THOUGH...
...YOU'RE HAVING SOME TROUBLE OVER HERE...

READ
THIS
WAY

SAKURA...
YOU
GUYS
DID IT...

YES...
BUT...
WHERE'S
GAARA?

GLANCE

...GOOD
...

...

I CAN'T BELIEVE IT...
SASORI GOT TAKEN OUT BY THAT BRAT GIRL AND THE OLD BAT...

READ THIS WAY

GOOD JOB, NEJI.
TA-DAA

!
!

KA-CHING

THUNK THUNK THUNK THUNK THUNK

I WON'T BE ABLE TO OUTRUN THEM.

GUY'S TEAM...?

READ THIS WAY

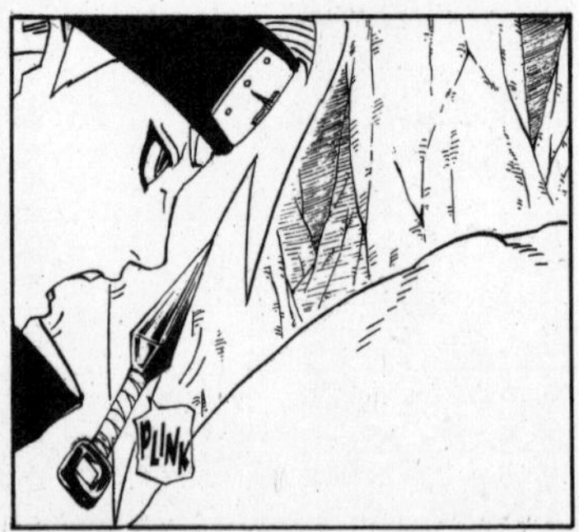

SHWIP

LET ME SHOW YOU MY ULTIMATE ART...
IT'S AN EXPLOSION!
PUFF
PUFF
TAK

!!

SHREEEE
ALL HIS CHAKRA IS CONCEN-TRATING ON ONE POINT...!
OH NO...

READ
THIS
WAY

EVERY-
ONE,
GET
OUT OF
HERE!!

!!

WHOOSH

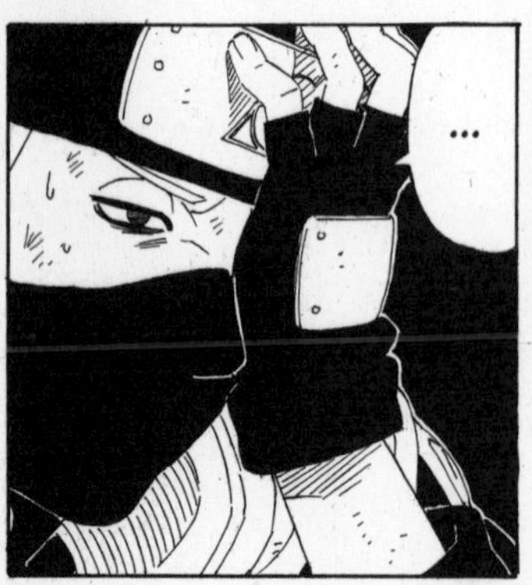
...

YEEAAGH

NARUTO

Number
278:
The Death of Gaara

BOOM

READ
THIS
WAY

WE'RE NOT GONNA MAKE IT!

ZOOM

FSSSH

...

...!

WHAT'S GOING ON?

...

...

...!

ZZZH

!

ZIP
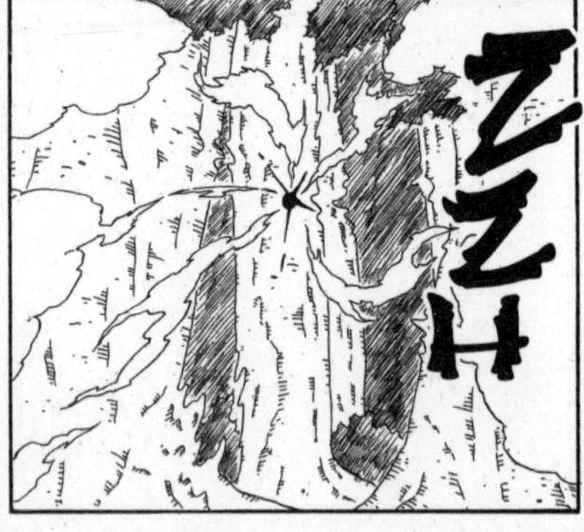
ZZZH

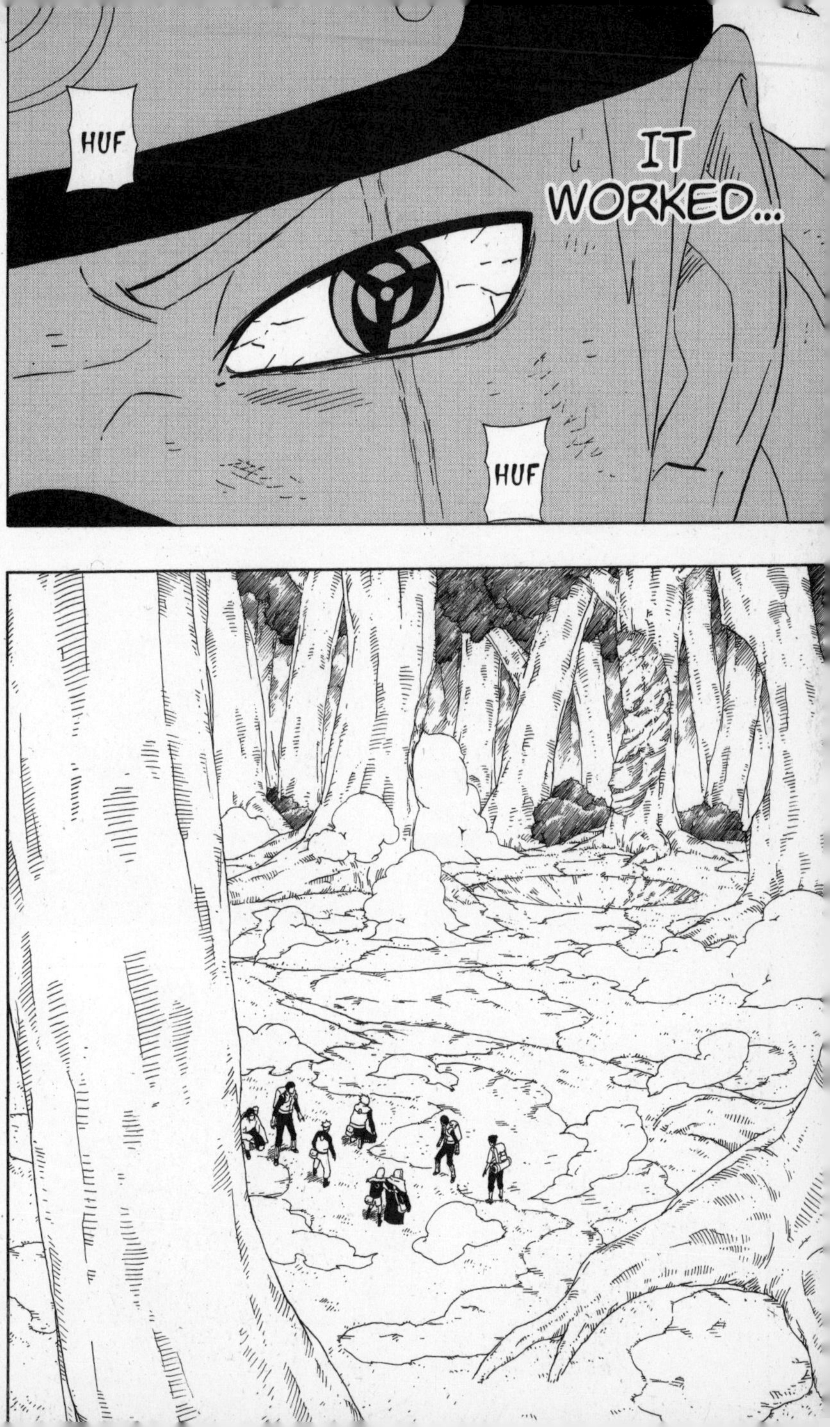

HUF
IT WORKED...
HUF

READ THIS WAY

...

HUF
HUF

...A WORTHY RIVAL...

!
STAGGER

FWUMP
MASTER KAKASHI?!

...WHAT ON EARTH...
...DID YOU DO...?

I TELE-PORTED HIM...
...AND THE EXPLOSION TO ANOTHER SPACE...
HUF
HUF

STAK
!

IS EVERYONE OKAY...?
NEVER MIND THAT...

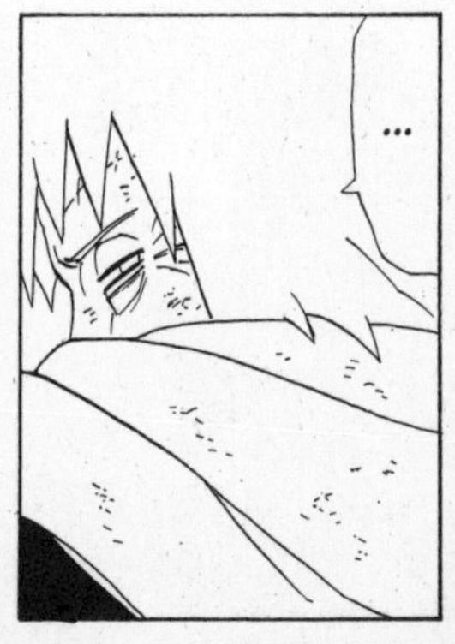
...

...
YUP

SAKURA...

...SAKURA.
...
...

SHF

...

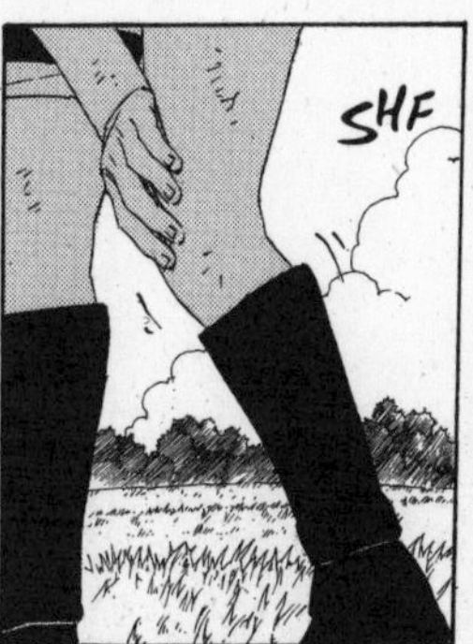
SHF

READ
THIS
WAY

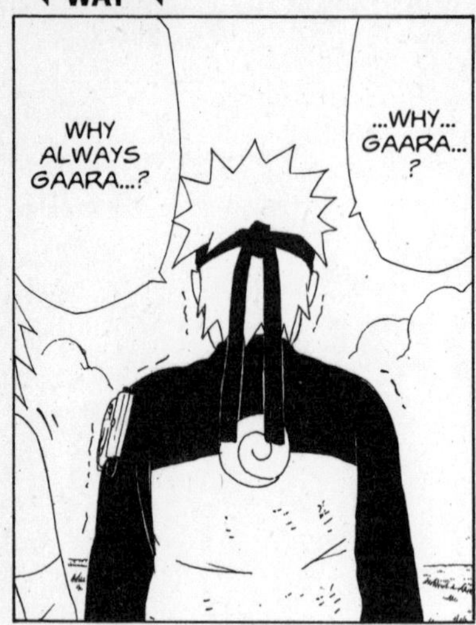
...WHY... GAARA... ?
WHY ALWAYS GAARA...?

IF HE DIES LIKE THIS...!
CLENCH

HE'S KAZEKAGE...

HE'S JUST BECOME KAZEKAGE...

CALM DOWN...
UZUMAKI NARUTO...

SHUT
UP!!!

...

IF YOU SAND NINJA...
...HADN'T PUT THAT MONSTER IN GAARA...
...NONE OF THIS WOULD HAVE HAPPENED!!!

DID YOU EVER EVEN CONSIDER WHAT GAARA THOUGHT?!
DID YOU EVER EVEN ASK?!!

...YOU CALL HIM A JINCHÛRIKI HOST?!!

WHO ARE YOU TO DECIDE THAT FATE FOR SOMEONE ELSE?!!

READ THIS WAY

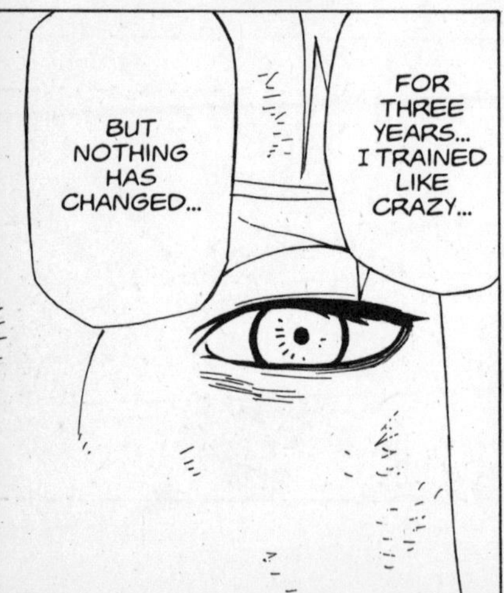

...

SKF

TMP
TMP

SHF

FWOO

READ
THIS
WAY

HOOOOOM

!!

...!

GRANNY
CHIYO...
THAT
JUTSU...!!

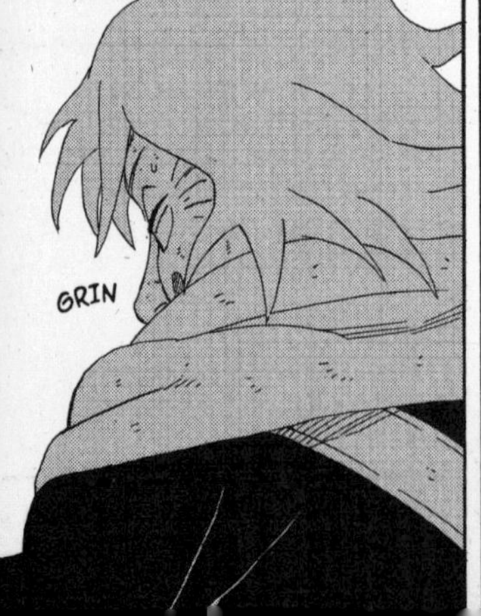
GRIN

GRANNY CHIYO...

...WHAT'S SHE DOING?

MEDICAL NINJUTSU...?
NO...

THERE'S STILL...
...SOMETHING I MUST DO...

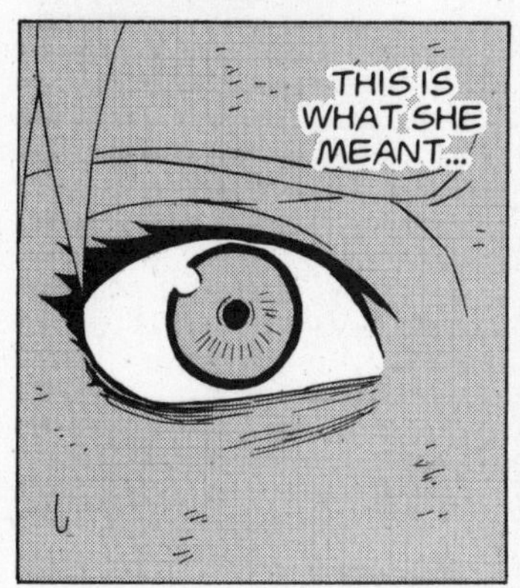
THIS IS WHAT SHE MEANT...

IN EXCHANGE FOR HER LIFE...

READ THIS WAY

SHE'S GOING TO...

...BRING GAARA BACK!!

NARUTO

Number 279: Power & Miracles...!!

READ THIS WAY

...COMMEN-
SURATE
RISK...

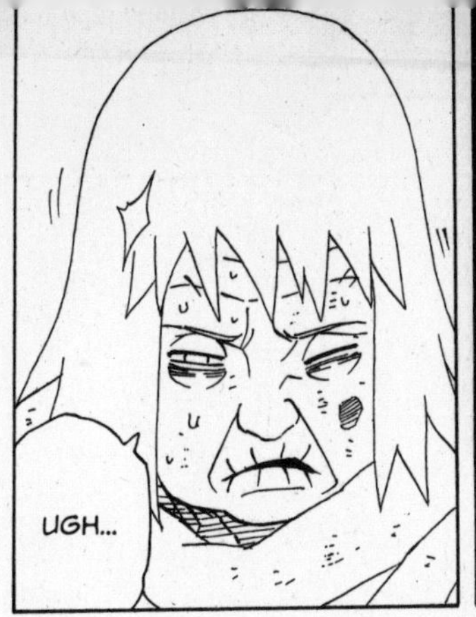
UGH...

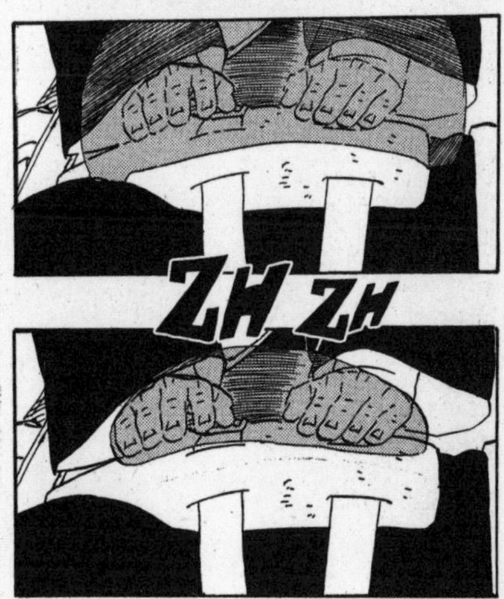
ZH ZH

NO...!
NOT
ENOUGH
CHAKRA.

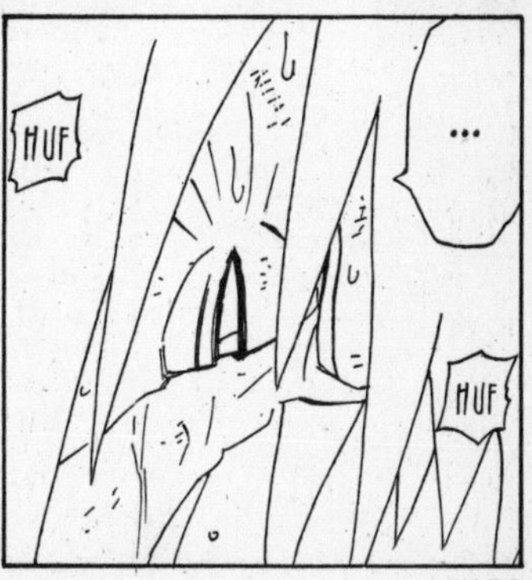
HUF
...
HUF

!
PLEASE...
USE MY
CHAKRA...!

READ THIS WAY

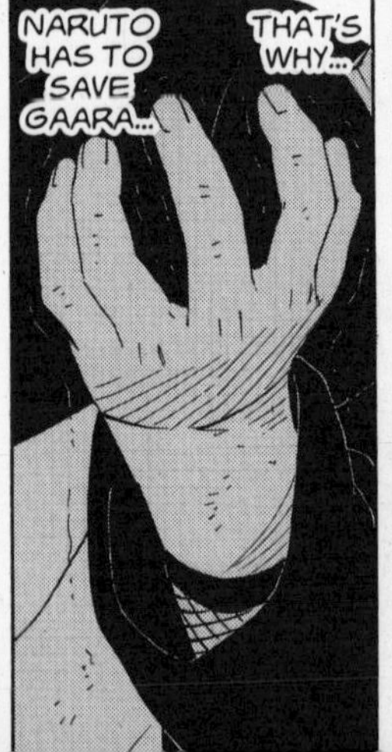

PLACE YOUR HANDS ON MINE.
!

...

SHF
SHF

NOD

CRACKLE
...

NARUTO...
...

READ
THIS
WAY

...

NARUTO'S DREAM IS TO BECOME HOKAGE...
SO WHEN HE HEARD THAT GAARA BECAME KAZEKAGE IT FRUSTRATED HIM.

BUT, ON THE OTHER HAND, NARUTO WAS SINCERELY HAPPY FOR GAARA.
NARUTO POSSESSES A SPECIAL POWER.

HUF
WITHOUT EXCHANGING MANY WORDS...
HUF
HE CAN STRIKE UP A FRIENDSHIP WITH ANYONE...
HUF

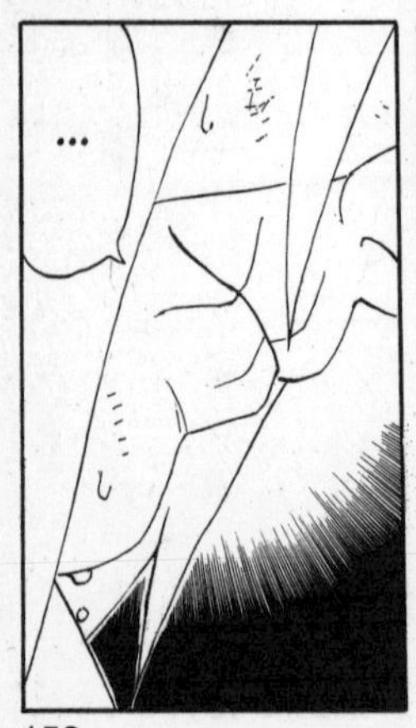
...

IN THIS SHINOBI WORLD CREATED BY FRIVOLOUS OLD PEOPLE...
...I'M GLAD NEW SOULS LIKE YOU HAVE COME ALONG...

...!

UP 'TIL NOW...
...EVERYTHING I'VE DONE HAS BEEN WRONG...

...BUT... AT THE VERY END...
...I THINK I MIGHT FINALLY BE ABLE TO DO SOMETHING RIGHT.

SUNA AND...

KONOHA...

READ THIS WAY

...

MAY THEIR FUTURE BE...
...SOMETHING DIFFERENT FROM OUR TIME...

THIS SPECIAL POWER OF YOURS...
...KAKASHI SPOKE OF IT...
THAT POWER WILL CHANGE THE FUTURE DRAMATI-CALLY...
BECOME A HOKAGE THE LIKE OF WHICH HAS NEVER BEEN SEEN!

AND SAKURA... IN THE FUTURE, DON'T SAVE A DYING GRANNY LIKE ME...
...HELP THOSE YOU TRULY CARE ABOUT...

YOU'RE... A LOT LIKE ME...

SO FEW WOMEN POSSESS SUCH STRONG SPIRIT...
YOU'LL LIKELY SURPASS YOUR TEACHER...

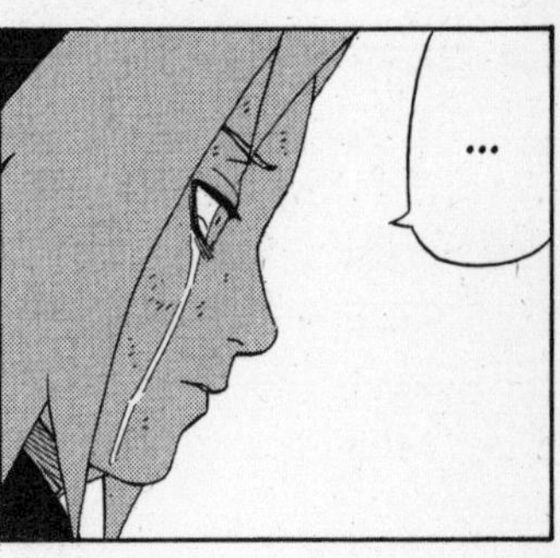
...

NARUTO...
I HAVE A FAVOR TO ASK...
!

YOU'RE THE ONLY PERSON WHO KNOWS...
...GAARA'S PAIN...

GAARA ALSO KNOWS *YOUR* PAIN...

READ THIS WAY

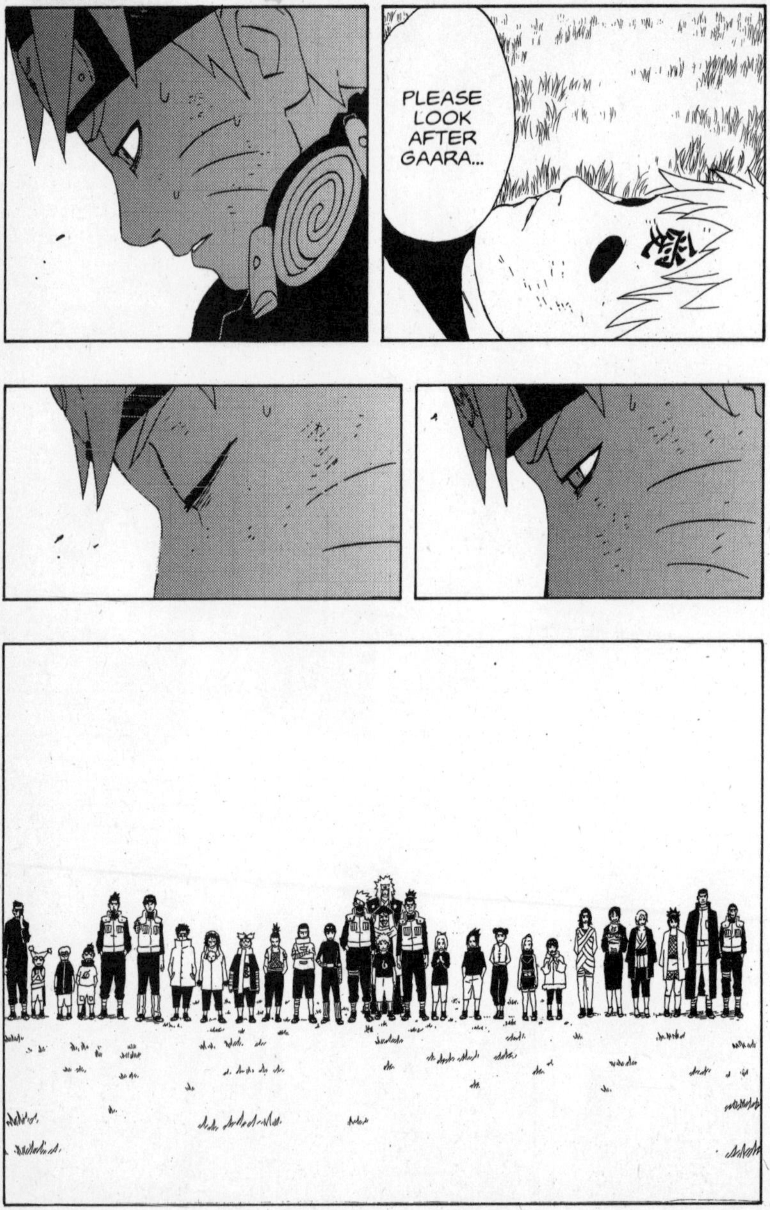

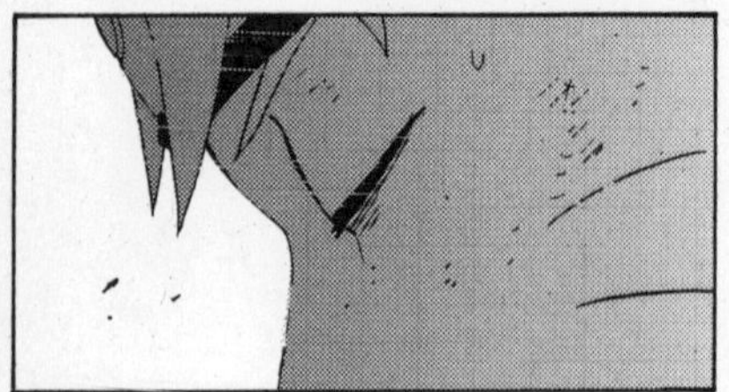

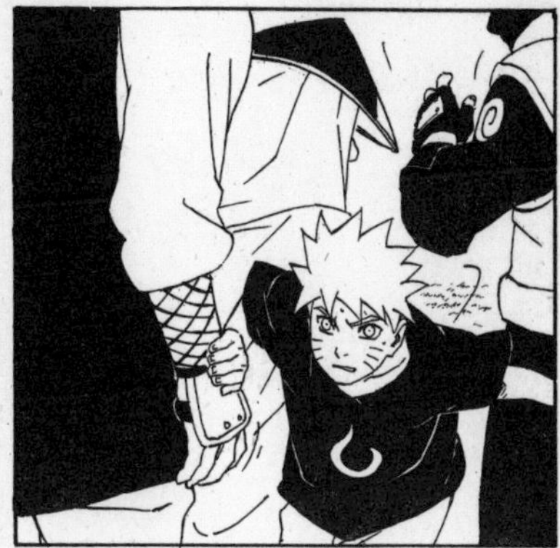

GAARA!

READ
THIS
WAY

...WHO...?
...WHO...IS
HE
CALLING?

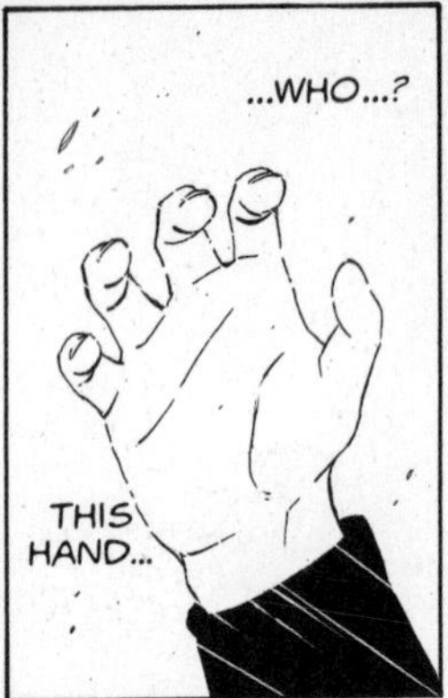
...WHO...?
THIS
HAND...

OH...
IT'S MY
HAND
AGAIN...

...MY HAND...
...ME...?

READ
THIS
WAY

ME...
WHO...AM
I...?

I'M...

TAP

...GAARA...

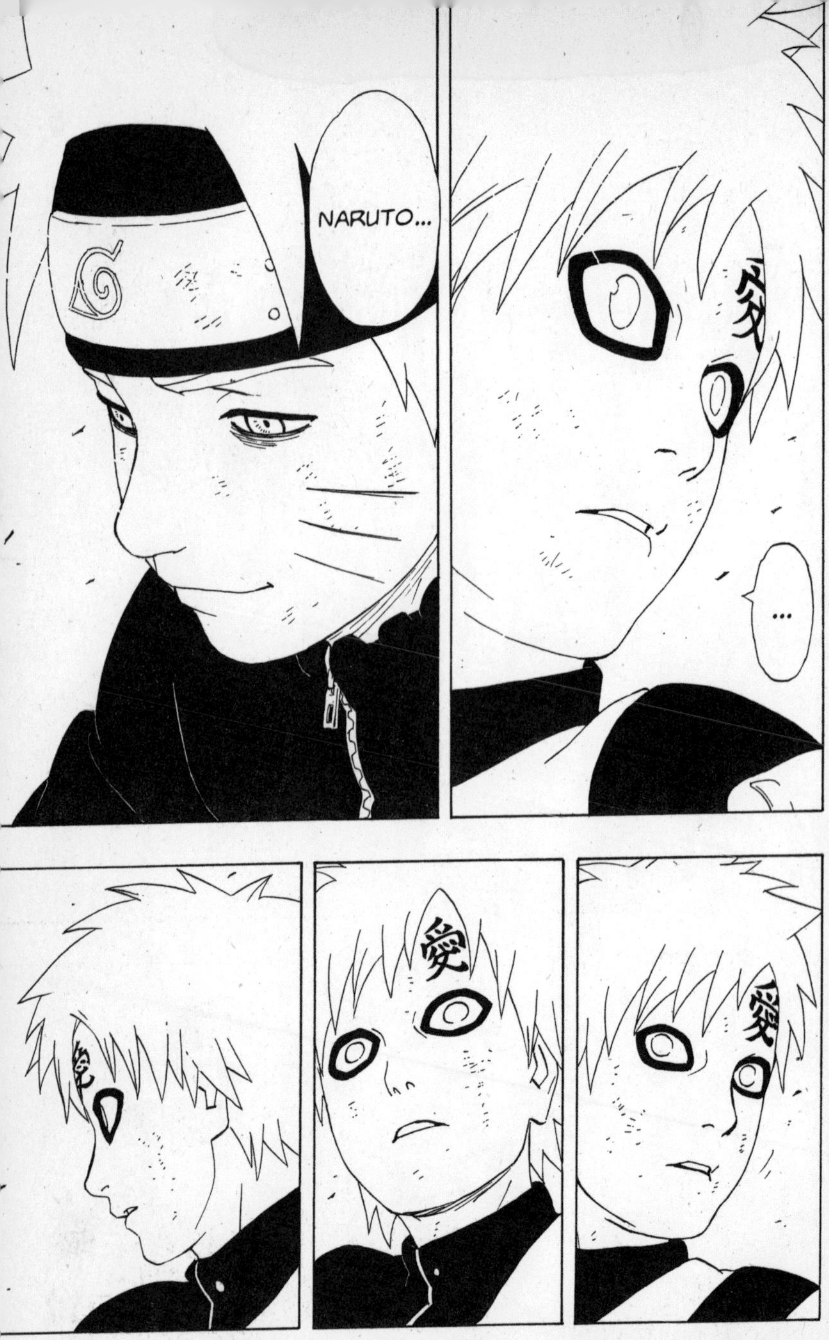

...

NARUTO...

...WHAT'S THIS...?
WE ALL CAME RUNNING...
...TO YOUR RESCUE...

GRATITUDE FOR FAN MAIL

THANKS, EVERYONE, VERY MUCH FOR ALL YOUR FAN MAIL. I ALWAYS CREATE MY MANGA IN MY ROOM, NEVER KNOWING HOW READERS FEEL ABOUT IT. SO, BECAUSE FAN MAIL IS THE ONLY WAY I CAN COMMUNICATE WITH MY READERS, I'M REALLY HAPPY TO RECEIVE YOUR LETTERS. I READ YOUR LETTERS WHENEVER I HAVE TIME. SOME PEOPLE DOUBT WHETHER I REALLY READ THEM OR NOT, AND WANT ME TO PROVE THAT I DO. BUT DON'T WORRY. I REALLY AM READING THEM. I WISH I COULD WRITE BACK. HOWEVER, I RECEIVE SO MUCH THAT IF I WROTE BACK, I WOULDN'T HAVE TIME LEFT TO DO MY MANGA. THAT'S NOT THE WAY I'D LIKE IT, BUT I WANT TO MAKE UP FOR NOT REPLYING AND SHOW MY GRATITUDE BY CREATING MORE AND MORE INTERESTING MANGA. AFTER ALL, IF MY MANGA ISN'T INTERESTING, YOU'LL STOP SENDING FAN MAIL (*LAUGH*). FOR THOSE OF YOU WHO WROTE TO ME, I'LL KEEP TRYING TO CREATE MANGA THAT YOU'LL ENJOY!

I HOPE YOU'LL CONTINUE TO SUPPORT *NARUTO*!

MASASHI KISHIMOTO

Number 280: Trust!!

YOU HAD US WORRIED...!

...

HMPH
YOU SURE DID.
YOU CAUSED US A TON OF GRIEF, LITTLE BROTHER.
!

DON'T ACT SO SUPERIOR!
GAARA IS KAZEKAGE.
SHUT ALL YOUR MOUTHS!

READ
THIS
WAY

YOU BRATS!

...GAARA... HOW ARE YOU FEELING?
GASP

PAT

UGH...
UHN

...YOU SHOULDN'T MOVE TOO SUDDENLY.
YOUR BODY HASN'T COMPLETELY RECOVERED FROM THE RIGOR MORTIS YET.

SOB... SOB... WHAT A RELIEF...
I THOUGHT LORD KAZEKAGE WAS REALLY GONE...

LORD GAARA WOULDN'T DIE SO EASILY!!
THAP
OUCH!

LORD GAARA IS A SILENT, COOL, STRONG AND HANDSOME ELITE WARRIOR...
YES, YES. AND HE'S CUTE TOO, BUT HE'S KAZEKAGE...

I'LL PROTECT YOU FROM YOUR ENEMIES NEXT TIME!
NO, I WILL!
BUMP
ZOOM

ZOOP
...COME TO THINK OF IT, I'M STILL A GENIN...

HEY, CHEER UP...
GIRLS ARE ALWAYS ATTRACTED TO COOL, ELITE TYPES.
SHF
!

I THINK... SHIKAMARU SAID SOMETHING LIKE THAT TOO...
HMM...
FUP

HE'S...
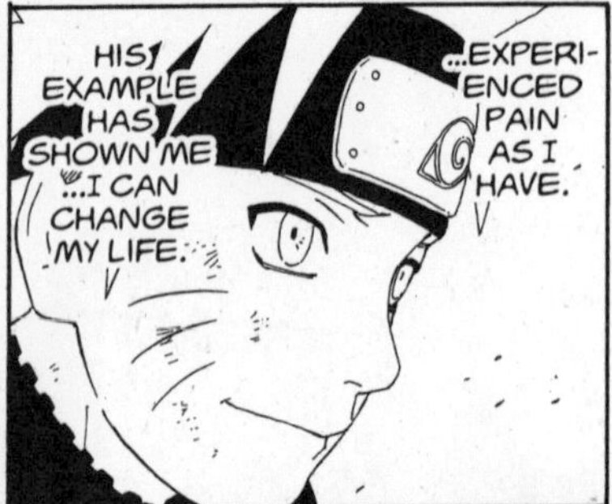
...EXPERI-ENCED PAIN AS I HAVE.
HIS EXAMPLE HAS SHOWN ME ...I CAN CHANGE MY LIFE.

THANKS... NARUTO.
!
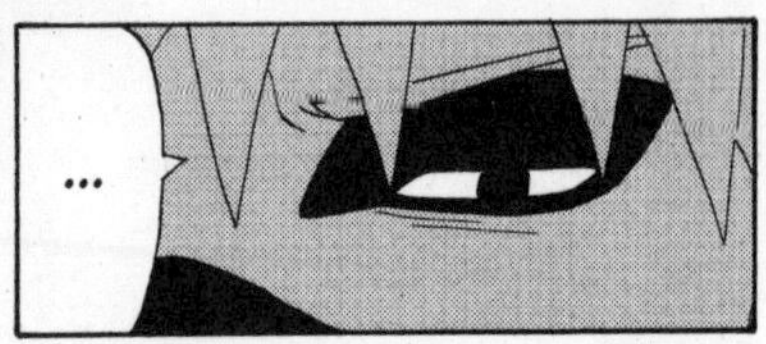
...
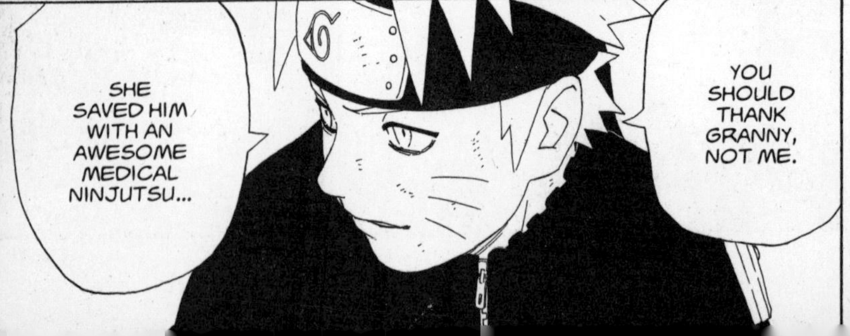
YOU SHOULD THANK GRANNY, NOT ME.
SHE SAVED HIM WITH AN AWESOME MEDICAL NINJUTSU...

DID GRANNY CHIYO... USE THAT JUTSU...?

SHE WAS TIRED AND FELL ASLEEP...

BUT SHE'LL BE FINE WHEN SHE GETS HOME...

NO...

?!

IT WASN'T MEDICAL NINJUTSU. IT WAS A TRANSFERENCE TECHNIQUE...

GRANNY CHIYO IS DEAD.

READ THIS WAY

IN THIS SHINOBI WORLD CREATED BY FRIVOLOUS OLD PEOPLE... I'M GLAD NEW SOULS LIKE YOU HAVE COME ALONG...

UP UNTIL NOW...EVERYTHING I'VE DONE HAS BEEN WRONG...
...BUT... AT THE VERY END... I THINK I MIGHT FINALLY BE ABLE TO DO SOMETHING RIGHT.

SUNA AND... KONOHA...
MAY THEIR FUTURE BE... SOMETHING DIFFERENT FROM OUR TIME...

THIS SPECIAL POWER OF YOURS... KAKASHI SPOKE OF IT...
THAT POWER WILL CHANGE THE FUTURE DRAMATICALLY...

BECOME A HOKAGE THE LIKE OF WHICH HAS NEVER BEEN SEEN!

READ
THIS
WAY

GRANNY CHIYO...

SHE LOOKS LIKE SHE'LL JUST LAUGH AND SAY...
...I WAS JUST PRETEND-ING...
...HMM...

SHE LOOKS SO PEACEFUL...

SHF

...
...YES...
PLIP

愛

...

NARUTO... LIKE I THOUGHT, YOU'RE DEFINITELY DIFFERENT.
YOU HAVE THE POWER TO CHANGE PEOPLE...

READ THIS WAY

愛

愛

SHF...
LORD GAARA...
I'M FINE...

FUP

...

...!

...EVERY-
ONE.
PRAY
FOR
GRANNY
CHIYO.

CRACK

CRACK CRACK

BAM

PHEW!

...

HMMM...
I ONLY LOST MY ARM FROM THE ELBOW...
I HAVE TO FIND MY RIGHT HAND AND THE RING I DROPPED...

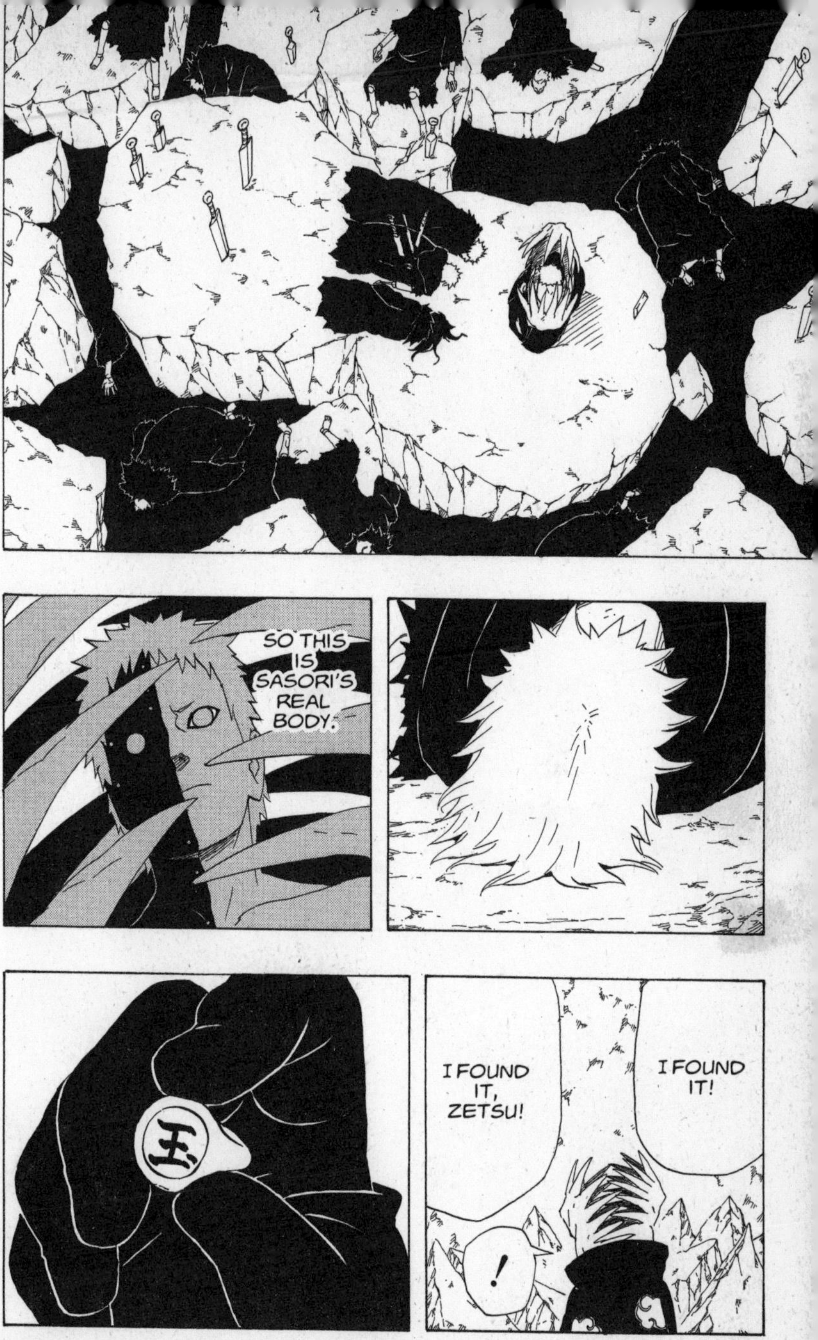

SO THIS IS SASORI'S REAL BODY.

I FOUND IT!
I FOUND IT, ZETSU!
!
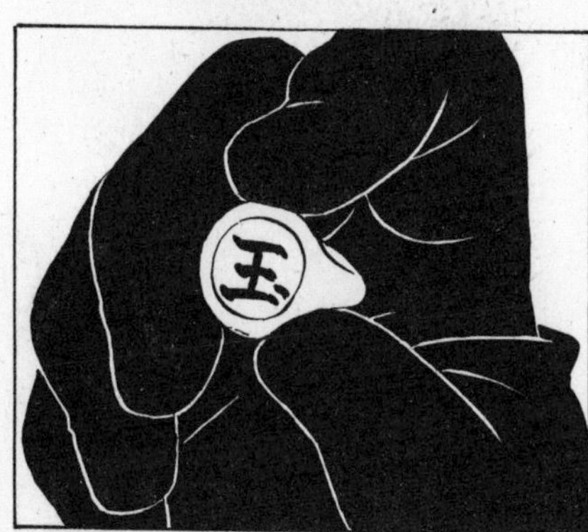

WILL THIS BE ENOUGH FOR ME TO JOIN THE AKATSUKI...?
FLIP
THERE'S NOW AN OPENING FOR ONE...
FOOL... IT'S NOT THAT EASY...
WHY NOT...? LET HIM JOIN...
TOBI'S A GOOD BOY...
WHOOPS ...
SHUP
TO BE CONTINUED IN NARUTO VOL.32!

IN THE NEXT VOLUME...

THE SEARCH FOR SASUKE

A new ninja joins the ranks of Team Kakashi! What does he hide behind his unassuming smile? And will he ever be able to live up to the reputation of the powerful ninja he replaces—Sasuke?!

AVAILABLE NOVEMBER 2008!

Read it first in SHONEN JUMP magazine!

Complete you
collection with t
NARUTO books,
anime TV series,
and OVA
SHONEN JUMP™
NARUTO™
THE MOVIE
Ninja Clash in the Land of Snow
Naruto's just gotten his dream assignment: guarding his favorite actress, Yukie Fujikaze, as she shoots the final scenes of her latest movie in the Land of Snow. But the set isn't the only thing that's frigid—can Naruto and his team warm up to their demanding star and the not-so-friendly locals?
Find out in *Naruto The Movie: Ninja Clash in the Land of Snow*—own it on DVD today!
SHONEN JUMP
THE WORLD'S MOST POPULAR MANGA
Visit www.naruto.com for online games, downloads, and more!
© 2002 MASASHI KISHIMOTO © NMP 2004
RATED T FOR TEEN
ratings.viz.com
VIZ media
www.viz.com

SJ
NARUTO
THE OFFICIAL FANBOOK
RATED
T
FOR
TEEN
ratings.viz.com
VIZ media
www.viz.com

NARUTO VOL. 31
The SHONEN JUMP Manga Edition

This graphic novel contains material that was originally published in English in **SHONEN JUMP** #67-68. Artwork in the magazine may have been slightly altered from that presented here.

STORY AND ART BY MASASHI KISHIMOTO

Translation/Kyoko Shapiro, HC Language Solutions, Inc.
English Adaptation/Ian Reid, HC Language Solutions, Inc.
Consultant/Mari Morimoto
Touch-up Art & Lettering/Inori Fukuda Trant
Design/Sean Lee
Editor/Joel Enos

Editor in Chief, Books/Alvin Lu
Editor in Chief, Magazines/Marc Weidenbaum
VP of Publishing Licensing/Rika Inouye
VP of Sales/Gonzalo Ferreyra
Sr. VP of Marketing/Liza Coppola
Publisher/Hyoe Narita

Printed in the U.S.A.

Published by VIZ Media, LLC
P.O. Box 77010
San Francisco, CA 94107

SHONEN JUMP Manga Edition
10 9 8 7 6 5 4 3 2 1
First printing, September 2008

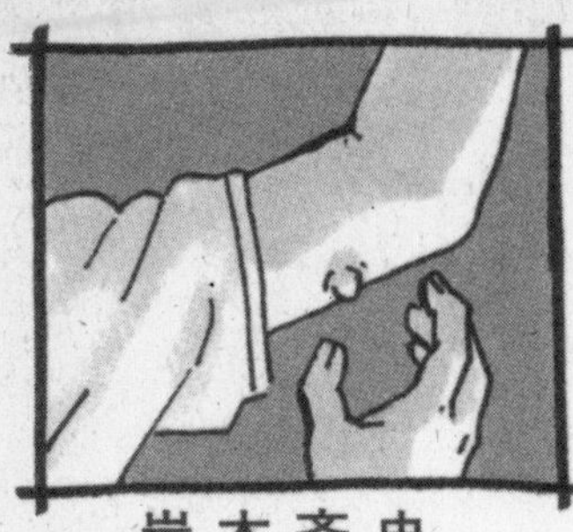

岸本斉史

Recently I carelessly plucked a wart off of my upper arm. Gouging it out left that part of my skin damaged with a depression in it. The whole thing left me with a different kind of depression.

—Masashi Kishimoto, 2005

Author/artist Masashi Kishimoto was born in 1974 in rural Okayama Prefecture, Japan. After spending time in art college, he won the Hop Step Award for new manga artists with his manga **Karakuri** (Mechanism). Kishimoto decided to base his next story on traditional Japanese culture. His first version of **Naruto**, drawn in 1997, was a one-shot story about fox spirits; his final version, which debuted in **Weekly Shonen Jump** in 1999, quickly became the most popular ninja manga in Japan.